The
Operating Manual
to Life

The
Operating Manual
to Life

BREAKING LOOPS

Healing and Conscious Evolution

David Dayan Fisher

ISBN: 9798298316859

Cover Design by Patricia Krebs
Book design by Wordzworth.com

Retep Nap Creations

Author's Note

I will continually repeat myself in this book, as I did in the last book, to increase the potential of the messages' ability to be ingested and digested at a far deeper level.

It would assist and serve these words to have first read my book *The Map.*

Life is a process of returning to our truth, remembering, resolving, dissolving, evolving, elevating, regulating, and resonating higher and higher within. This process is a practice. The practice is a courageous, determined discipline of facing the self in every moment of every moment. This is the hero's journey, and it never ends; it just climbs into even more clarity, ease, and peace.

Life Is a School

You have a unique curriculum set out for you from before birth. You will meet people and have specific lessons and teachers along the way. You will constantly be presented with potential opportunities to learn, grow, and evolve consciously. This is your karmic journey. This is what they label as spiritual work, healing work. I call it conscious evolution, breaking loops.

This is the Evolutionist's School of life. We are all Evolutionists.

This book is just a perception. How you decide to utilize it is your choice.

With humble gratitude, I dedicate this book to my own courage and discipline, as well as all the greatest teachers of my life, past and present.

The Author
David Dayan Fisher

D avid has experienced a roller-coaster wonder of his own journey through life. From his parents' hellish divorce when he was three, hiding in dark places hoping the violence wouldn't find him, wishing he were dead, to all the twists and turns and ups and downs that got him to where he is now.

With much of what they label as trauma, physical and emotional, he traveled the hide-and-seek of life to finally crumble and go within to find what he couldn't find outside.

Expelled from Hebrew classes, Cub Scouts, and high school for violence, he then went on to drug taking and dealing in London's clubland. Hedonism was his religion. After suffering some serious side effects of taking so many drugs, he decided to heal himself with clean food, fitness, and walking away from the scene and people that fed his mayhem. He cleaned up his life, and at the same time found his passion in the world of acting.

He trained at the Royal Central School of Speech and Drama, went to improv classes, and joined a theater company, all while working in event catering as well as auditioning and doing commercials, bit parts, and pop videos.

In 2001 he moved to Los Angeles and continued with his dream. After four years he got his break in the hit movie *National Treasure*. He also achieved success and recognition in other worldwide movies and TV shows such as *NCIS*. He always played the villain, the bad guy, killing many and dying many times. He then began his other dream to write books and movie screenplays and to paint.

As time moved along, now with his two newfound rescue dogs and the sudden death of his mother, his mild fame and fortune never seemed to be enough. He had started drinking again, and anger began to surface. This was the catalyst to dive inward. Continuing his acting, he started to read Eckhart Tolle's books and then became greatly interested in the deeper mechanics of human behavior. Now, with nearly two decades of studying motives and emotions in acting, he delved even further into the depths of the ego identity, the soul's perceptions, and all of the labels of consciousness and spirituality.

In 2017, he left the circus of Hollywood and moved to a small canyon town outside of Los Angeles to focus on his art and writing. He soon met a lady who was his muse and catalyst to enroll in a college to study spiritual psychology. There, he studied, lived, and worked with his partner in doing as much inner work as he could, as best he could. All his childhood wounds and trauma began to surface. Unable, and not fully educated with the deeper understanding and tools needed, to see clearly and heal, his relationship fell apart.

It was then that he made the decision to dive even deeper, to become the best possible version of himself, dedicating his life to the study and healing of his now resurfacing darkness and pain.

He studied with numerous masters and teachers; took courses here, there, and everywhere; read non-stop; and cried, wailed, and died again and again. Delving into the experience of his own hidden pain, and moving into it and through it, was now his passion and priority. But it also meant figuring out as much about why we as humans have come to this place and space in human consciousness.

This has now become his purpose in life. David has published and written numerous fiction books and kids' books, as well as his ever-growing best-selling book, *The Map*. He is also an avid screenwriter, with eight finished movies, and loves to paint his bubblegum pop art around the word *love*.

In this book, he shares as much as possible, to give others the tools and understandings to transform their own lives to a deeper degree.

Reading and studying are just intellectual knowledge, ten miles apart from the actualizing of ingesting, digesting, metabolizing, utilizing, and embodying each moment of each moment in the experiment and experience of life.

David continues on his own journey, evolving in his own inward and upward travels, doing the work, facing himself, moment to moment, as well as sharing all he can on Instagram and assisting others in his personal and very unique one-on-one Evolutionist sessions.

Disclaimer

The information presented is the author's opinion and does not constitute any health or medical advice. The content of this book is for informational purposes only and is not intended to diagnose, treat, cure, or prevent any condition or disease.

Please seek advice from your health-care provider for your personal health concerns prior to taking health-care advice from this book.

Instructions

As you read or listen to this book, be conscious and aware of your breathing, making it deeper and slower than normal.

Contents

Introduction

Hopefully, by now, you've read my book *The Map*, the translation and navigation to life and the human experience, and have a greater understanding of how, what, and why you got to be how you are. I made that book as easy to ingest as I could. And I'm going to do the same with this one. Breaking loops is a simplified word for what is known as the awakening process, spirituality, healing, regulating the nervous system, conscious evolution, emotional regulation, inner work, or in lightening the self.

Labels are just labels. We are simply a constructed ethereal, energetic factory of emotions, feelings, thoughts, beliefs, and narratives that loop our life into itself, thinking we are the loops, feeling we are the loops, believing we are the loops, and perceiving and narrating life through the lenses of these loops. These are simply a well-practiced, well-acted constant of our constructed software that literally keeps updating itself by downloading and re coding itself into the same old same, by our being who and how we are, constantly, unconsciously, unaware, moment to moment.

I am only experiencing me.

Only The Children Will Enter The Kingdom The Kingdom Is Within

All young children are free of the constructs of our adult insecurities and neuroses. They are mostly regulated in their nervous systems, to a degree. They have no judgments, no hurt, no pain, no limiting beliefs, no formed perceptions, no identifications of identity, no indoctrinations, no conditionings, and no programming. They are literally liberated of all of which an adult becomes. A young child is mostly in love and in joy. Then, as they grow, they start to build barriers, blocks, and bricks to this truth in the ethereal form of loops.

The systems in place, example, suggest, inform, indoctrinate, and program by stealth, as the human operating system in-forms itself, downloads and codes itself, with no real education but the blindness and dysfunction of others around it.

The child's innocence and authenticity start to turn to fear and survival, as an unsafe, unsure, insecure performance anxiety takes hold. The child is now interpreting without an interpreter; translating without an operating manual; and navigating without map, rudder, or sail. They live with that of which is experienced and modeled by others. The kingdom within is now buried under a bag of darkness and weight. This is what we are in lightening ourselves of.

A child feels first. The child's nervous system in-forms itself through the language of the ethers of energy, emotions, and feelings. It codes and downloads and loops these feelings constantly. Then, after time, it learns language and creates stories about these feelings, and then it simply interprets, believes, understands, and then perceives through these narratives, this language. Actually, they misinterpret, create limiting beliefs, misunderstand, and then misperceive and see through these lenses as the child grows up.

Life Is a Jounrey
of Evolving

*E*volve. The word actually expresses itself within itself. The first four letters spell love backwards. We are evolving back to love. We are dissolving our default settings and returning to our factory setting. This is the very essence of our truth. And it is this truth that sets us free.

The child inside is free. This is where our kingdom waits for us. The hero's journey moves through the old pain and old hurt and clears all the lenses of our old false perceptions. This is, to me, what life is about. This is a lifelong moment to moment journey of regulating, elevating, and evolving. When one person travels back to love, they resonate and shine their light to assist others. And so, it continues to change the collective, the world, and humanity.

This is how we all evolve. This is how humanity evolves.

My life is no different to others'. I have traveled a long way to get to here, how I am, where I am within me, and I am continuing along the way. This is a whole new way of living, a new language to life, a new operating system, a new navigation and translation of the human experience.

The Wounded Child Inside

(This is just a descriptive phrase, a narrative of stuck ethereal and emotional loops.)

Every single hit, beating, hurt, shout, scorn, judgment, criticism, and belittling statement is felt by a child. Every time a parent releases their temper, their impatience, their frustrations, their inability to emotionally regulate, as well as the constant performance pressure, the child feels it, energetically, and interprets it into language. The child has zero understanding or capability to know anything but to feel and think that they are unsafe, unloved, not good enough, unworthy, undeserving, bad, wrong, stupid, and not important. The pain of the unloved self is formed inside most of us to varying degrees. I call it the ten thousand wounds. And this hurt and pain become our self-perceptions, the lenses we see through. These stuck feelings and thoughts all operate alongside our ethereal, emotional, mental, and biological operating systems. We then grow up and protect them; we simply don't want to feel the hurt and pain again. We do anything we can to either soothe or overcompensate to try to change the feelings from outside of us. We can wallow in them or try to outrun them or escape them or become something to alter them, achieve, attain, and even marry or become famous to not feel the discomfort, the unease, the restlessness, the emptiness, and the loneliness of it all.

As a child, I constantly felt the unloved feelings, the shame, the pain, again and again and again, repeating in my head and body how unloved, unsafe, stupid, bad, wrong, and not good enough I was, looping and downloading the same old same words, thoughts, and feelings. I was cementing and creating my very own operating systems of beliefs, dysregulations, and perceptions. I was the cause of my own effect, my deep, unaware, unconscious looping hurt and pain.

No matter what, we will always have these feelings attached to beliefs, narratives, and thoughts inside us until we actually face them and not wallow or run and hide from them.

We soothe, escape, numb, sedate, distract, and stimulate constantly to not feel them. This means we keep them, cement them, loop them, and never face them or feel them, move through them, dissolve them, or heal them. That is our very dis-ease.

Inner Child

All that is not of love or loving is for us to face, to feel, to heal. We wanted to be seen, met, listened to, loved, and understood as kids. We wanted to be safe, validated, and accepted for us, as we were, not as others needed or wanted for them. And so, we simply created our homework for life, our unresolved issues, our limiting beliefs, and unmet needs. In the end, take out all the psychobabble and spiritual rhetoric and fad labels, and we are simply dealing with feelings. How I feel is the core of my consciousness.

When we feel unloved, unsafe, unworthy, not good enough, stupid, bad, wrong, shame, guilt, lesser than, it can be seen as all our old stuffed down stuff of our little child inside rising up. Other people and what they say or don't say, do or don't do, will mirror these feelings back to us. The trigger is inside, as is the ammunition. If there was no ammunition, there would be nothing to get triggered.

Examples

Someone cuts us off in traffic.

Someone is late.

A family member or close friend makes a joke or criticizes us.

The boss screams at us in front of others.

Our parents don't listen to us.

Our partner criticizes us, blames us, and judges us.

Someone wants to end a relationship.

We feel we can't do something or are at fault, that we made a mistake.

Each of these causes a reaction, a trigger inside. These will usually feel like shame, as well as a feeling of being unsafe, I'm not OK. The pain of shame does not want to be felt. How many times in our childhood did we feel shame, feel not good enough, unworthy, and unloved? We hold so much of the pain of shame inside us.

We sulked, we got punished, we got told, scolded, criticized, and felt, bad, wrong, and stupid. We hid inside ourselves, and we berated, narrated, and belittled ourselves again and again. Or we over-compensated to achieve, to feel more inside. This constant of stuck shame simply wanted to be loved and feel safe.

Now, in our adult life, this old shame presents itself when it's mirrored back to us, when it is trig-gered inside us, for us to face it, feel it, be with it, and move through its duration.

There is only us in here, experiencing us.

The narratives I usually create in my head, the narratives I direct at someone or something outside of me, the blames, complaints, judgments, and crit-icism, are all pointed outwardly and projected from my feelings inside of me, usually to protect feelings of shame or feeling unsafe.

Or there are my neurotic narratives I ramble about inside my head, about me, from me. This is all perpetuated as normal behaviors.

All my neurosis and insecurity, my impatience, my frustrations, my anxiety, my worry, my scarcity, my resentments, my hurt feelings, self-judgments, self-criticisms, hate, envy, jealousy, rage, and all else, are my potential homework to dissolve and resolve, to break their loops and patterns, to stop myself from recoding and downloading.

I have mostly been unaware of myself for much of my life and so, keep feeding my loops and not breaking them. This is the little boy or little girl of us all, continuing his or her subconscious downloads in adulthood. And it is this little child's feelings that keep being presented as opportunities, asking to be seen, to be met, to be sat with, to be felt and not avoided. All that upsets, disturbs, and is triggered inside us is our old stuff asking to be seen, met, felt, and moved through.

Conscious and Subconscious Loop

Your childhood formed your subconscious beliefs and programs along with the nervous system. These then play out and are birthed and looped again and again, as we think and feel, believe and perceive from our conscious mind repeating a loop that feeds and seeds itself. The conscious is the male seeding the subconscious, the female, and she births it all as the emotions drive it and loop with it. If we don't break our looping, we stay in our loops, repeating, seeding, and birthing the same old same.

The idea is to interrupt the loops, break them, stop seeding the subconscious with the unconscious conscious and so change the programs and patterns formed over much of our life. This is done by becoming aware and conscious of our unaware unconsciousness.

I code and download my feelings, narrate them, then loop them moment to moment with no regard or awareness that I'm the one doing this.

I am in forming me.

Re-Acting the Act of Our Loops

We react, re-acting the same reactions, acting the same act of us, thinking it's all about the outside world and other people. We also have feelings that arise from inside of us. We are simply thinking and feeling, while thinking and feeling it's just how we are. And we constantly allow them to be so, to grip us so. Here are the two major aspects of our looping:

1 The external world mirrors back our internal ammunition from childhood that triggers feelings and their reactions and narrations.
2 We keep feeling and looping our internal, rampant, unconscious, neurosis and insecurities.

Everything within us is a rinsed and repeated,

reacted, well-rehearsed performance of our method acts we've been unconscious and unaware of our whole lives. Waking up to this is what my life and books are all about. We act our act, react our reactions, looping the loops of their thoughts, feelings, and actions. We speak from how we are, think from how we are, and feel from how we are and don't even wake to see we are literally living in the past, repeating it, moment to moment.

How I am seemingly seems to be how I am. I just simply continue to accept how I experience life as it is, how I think it is, how I feel it is. It's not. It's how I am being, how I have become, a habitual constant I have constantly been inhabiting and choosing to be since my childhood.

If a Zen master can master all that is not Zen to become so, we have lived and practiced the process of our opposite, our stress, our worry, our impatience, our anxiety, our scarcity, our frustrations, and all else, becoming a doom and gloom master, a master of our misery, a victim to our inability, lost and blind to our full potential and far from our peace and contentment.

We also speak our words into a confirmed state, by stating how we are, believing how we are, make believing, narrating, and creating our very suffering, blindly looping our hypnotic broken emotional and mental broken record.

I'm so stressed, I'm anxious, I'm worried, I can't, and all else. We keep the script of our beliefs, feelings, and thoughts alive and that of our wounded childhood. We literally resonate and create a looping constant of each moment without knowing we are doing so. We have very little awareness and understanding that we can actually stop doing this.

We must realize that there is no magic pill, no hack, no quick fix to this system of self. Each of us is uniquely programmed into our own individual, specific curriculum in the school of life. We all have our own journey, with varying degrees of lessons to learn. Some might live looping a whole load of worry and yet have great patience. Some might have the ability to feel incredible abundance, while at the same time have much anxiety and insecurity about much else. Some might be a genius with one aspect and blindly ignorant in other ways. We all have many dimensions to our blindness and operating systems.

Life is a mirror showing me to me.

The First Awareness

There is, in actuality, nothing happening outside of me.

Other than my natural, instinctual fight-or-flight feelings of survival, I am also full of the bag of unloved, unsafe, not good enough ness, the hurt and pain of my childhood conditionings and patterns, my labeled wounds and traumas, my unresolved issues, my limiting beliefs, my unmet needs. These are the feelings I feel and thoughts that I think, the stories and narratives that I attach and make believe, that are far from loving and mostly neurotic and insecure.

The outside world, events, circumstances, situations, and other people are all simply being how they are, being and doing what they do. That's the what is of what is. How I am is the what is of how I am. And how I am is all my doing, my looping.

Knowing this is our first awareness. All that I feel is from within me, about me, for me to face, to sit with, to feel, for me to move through, for me to resolve, dissolve, regulate, elevate, heal from, and evolve, or what is known as breaking the loops of the past. This is what enlightenment is. To in lighten the self of all our old looping, re coding, and downloading mess, all our weight of emotional and mental baggage and stress, our neurosis and insecurities, and their shadows and darkness.

The Second Awarness

This is the awareness of becoming the watcher, the observer, the experiencer of the experience. Now, I am aware of me and of my feelings and thoughts. Now, I am starting the process and practice of detaching from my victim who thinks, believes, and perceives myself to be my thoughts, feelings, and experiences, as well as thinks the outside rules me, makes me feel and think the way I do. This is the first expansion of consciousness to a higher level from our normal blind unconscious unawareness that simply lives as we have done for most of our life, unaware. This awareness realization is not the same as embodying this higher position within the self. The understanding is not the same as actualizing. If I have been unaware my whole life, I am now set, like a software program, to play out the same act, the same loops, the same re actions, same thoughts, beliefs, feelings, and perceptions, because I'm literally habitually addicted to this blind way of being and seeing. No understanding, no intellectual knowledge can change these deep patterns and programmed ethereal loops; only the process of being and becoming the consciously aware and regulated loop breaker can.

My Operating Systems

I am a construct of my dysfunctions, dysregulation, and indoctrinations.

My hurt and pain, my labeled wounds, traumas, samskaras, karma, limiting beliefs, unresolved issues, unmet needs, neurosis, insecurities, protection mechanisms, preferences, and beliefs and perceptions all constructed around them, my emotions and feelings and thoughts of unworthiness, unsafe, unloved, not good enough, undeserving, not important, bad, wrong, stupid, and all else are the building blocks of my unconscious ego's identity, my character, and my personality, that all loop moment to moment.

I am a mental, neurological, psychological, emotional, biological, physiological, chemical, and ethereal operating system that works as one connected, creative universe, in unison, in a spiraling, looping bunch of behaviors, all of my own creation. They spiral around to loop around to spiral around to loop around, to no end, until I break my loops.

My dysfunctions of blindness, my lack, and operating systems perfectly join together with the programs and indoctrinations of the reward system, which have me believe that the outside will make me feel better, feel safe, will validate me, approve of me, accept me, love me, and make me feel good enough. And it is this wonderful mix of dysfunction, dysregulation, and indoctrinations that keeps me chasing, seeking, searching, needing, wanting, and trying to get, gain, and attain something or someone or go somewhere to change the feelings inside me.

The parenting and school systems, the media, the writers of books, TV, and movies all perpetuate the indoctrinations of life's fictions and fantasies that the outside will make the inside feel better, the outside will love your unloved parts, the outside will validate your lack inside. This is the greatest perpetuated delusion of being a human.

The Kingdom Is Within

This is referring to doing this work, working through all the dysfunction and dysregulations and returning to the factory setting. Only the children will enter the kingdom. The child is mostly free of dysfunction and indoctrination. We are to dissolve who we have become, to become who we already are, who we have always been under all the silliness of the constructs and building blocks of our childhood and operating systems that have been looping ever since. The pay for the work is a full and filled self, an abundance and brilliance of being love, joy, contentment, and peace.

Whatever I get from the outside will always mirror back to me how I am, how I feel, inside. This means no matter what I get, who I marry, how much money or fame, my dysfunction and dysregulation will soon enough be presented to me in how I feel. Then, normally, I just blame, criticize, complain, or need and seek and want for something else, something more, to overcompensate or try to soothe the pain of my unloved, unsafe, not good enough ness that is still looping, ruling, and fooling me.

Not enough ness can't be healed from the outside, from more.

The Third Awareness

The next awareness is that of the narratives in my head and the feelings behind them. The narratives are what we usually buy into, think is true, think is our reality. They are simply a perceived and projected, pointed, directed, scripted subjective reality. In other words, my blindness to what's actually happening, the feelings and where they come from.

I create, write, and script and act and believe these stories, words, neurosis, and insecurities moment to moment. I'm a habitual blind looping machine.

I feel, then react and attach a narrative, all in a blip of a second. The narratives are mostly pointing outwardly at others and the world. Or they are criticizing, judging, belittling, and berating myself from within me.

What happens is:

I have a feeling.

Then, within an instant, a blip, a split second, a narrative will join in and attach.

It seems like they are totally connected.

Then the narrative will either point outwardly, belittle, judge, criticize, blame, complain, react, snap, defend, or attack, or I will simply run a wallowing worry story, a scarcity story, an impatient or anxious story, a frustration narration, a well-rehearsed looping victim narrative.

It is the feeling that kicks it all into an instantaneous domino effect.

I fall into the feeling and attach and believe in the narrative.

This is my normal perceived reality and operating system. This is how I have been operating and perceiving my whole life. This is how everyone is. We loop this constant of our life constantly, moment to moment, unaware of its false operating programming.

What is actually happening is:

I am being presented with an old software program of my dysregulated nervous system stuck feelings, leftover loops from my past, old re coded downloaded stuff, my childhood, that I never stopped looping. These are usually the sufferings of my old emotional hurts and pains and all else that is connected to them. The external world is just a mirror, and the internal feelings I feel are simply reminding me, being triggered to what requires my attention.

Literally, all of our disturbs and upset, all that is triggered, that happens from inside me, is about me, from me, for me to regulate, to breathe, to face, to feel, to move through and break the loops.

Again and again, I have looped life, re acting the same old same, ignoring these potential opportunities.

I simply perpetuate the unconscious behaviors as normality. It is in fact quite dysfunctional and insane. We are repeating suffering, hurt and pain, without knowing it is being presented to alchemize and work through.

This is the simple basis of the operating systems of our old looping life. To break them takes a great strength of conscious awareness, a well-regulated nervous system, determination, discipline, and courage. This is why it's called the hero's journey. We literally face our dark demons, our self-inflicted habitual hurt and pain, our restless discomfort and unease, moment to moment, again and again, instead of normally deflecting and running from them, soothing them, or pointing from them like a victim. We have spent our whole life operating blind to this operating system.

Once was blind and now, I can see.

Moment to moment, I have opportunities being presented to me, for me to regulate, to practice my conscious awareness and dissolve and resolve the unresolved of the past. It's like a little child inside putting their hand up to say, "Hey, be here for my old pain, my old hurt, and help it feel seen, met, heard, and loved."

Self-love is simply not looping, not coding and downloading the unloved, dysregulated feelings, and not believing the unloving narratives moment to moment. This is the returning to our regulated truth, to love, to peace.

Educate, Regulate, and Elevate

First, we have to educate ourselves to understand the operating systems in place, to show us how our old systems have been continually and constantly downloading and looping themselves without our knowing. This is a deep deconstruction of the human experience and a slow but sure dissolving of all our behaviors, our identifications and attachments of our old operating systems.

We are now starting to learn to understand how humans have literally been blind to how to actually operate life. Our media perpetuates the unconscious. Looping life and reacting are written as normality. And so, the narratives of parenting, schools, and everyone in society reflect this in their behaviors, actions, reactions, thoughts, emotions, and words. It's the greatest spell of humanity that we all live in, thinking, believing, and perceiving it all to be how it is. It's not. We literally live asleep in life all the way to our last gasp. There is no wrong or right way. There is just the way you live, how you are within yourself. This is where compassion comes in.

Everyone is where they are, operating from their own loops, looping life, unknowingly. Forgive them for they know not that they loop.

The education is to know the truth of the self. As I expressed in *The Map*, we are simply an essence, a blank slate of consciousness, an awareness, a soul even, that has become clouded by our ego and life experiences, how we interpreted our childhood, created beliefs, perceptions, and dysregulations, and then think and feel and see through them. And these have all been continually experienced and looped unconsciously, repeating the same old same. This is the doing that has to be undone. These are the lenses of perception that have to be cleaned and cleared. These are the unresolved issues that need to be resolved and dissolved by us. These are the unmet needs we need to meet from within. These are the feelings we need to simply feel and move through. These are the loops we must break.

So, I educate myself to know thyself, to know that I have been blind, unconscious, and unaware. I educate myself to the understanding that I am now fully responsible and accountable for what is actually happening within the experience of my life, within me. This is learning to live with a new lens of perception. And while we are clearing and cleaning these lenses, we also have to see that mostly all others around us are not doing this, not knowing this, and don't care to know. This is our very own journey. And we must be gentle and compassionate with ourselves for where we are, as well as have compassion for where everyone else is.

The Map is an education in a nut shell. It's a great evolutionary leap to shift our consciousness, to face ourselves.

The most important understanding of this whole new journey of life is that it is a never-ending process of using the map, navigating and translating, and practicing breaking the loops. It does get easier, and it does happen quicker. It's creating a new nature of our second nature. It's like learning to live again, learning a new language, a new operating system, while the old one keeps trying to loop the past.

Our loops have been formed over our whole life. They are embedded into the ethers of our emotions, mentally, biologically, physiologically, psychologically, chemically, into all our operating systems.

Your neurological pathways are dug in and set but not in stone.

Your subconscious programs and patterns practiced, perfected, and preferred but can be reprogrammed.

Your nervous system is set to the familiar of its dysregulation to keep you surviving how it knew as a child, but can be regulated to become much more content, calm, and at peace.

And your body chemistry is habitually addicted to all the reactions, upsets, disturbs, triggers, neurosis, and insecurities of the past that just loop themselves again and again, releasing a soup of stress, a wonder of worry, a sack of scarcity, and much else emotionally and mentally, chemically enhanced. This is an addiction that can be broken.

We are a thinking, mental, feeling, emotional, ethereal energetic being.

So now we are educated to what is going on. We have played out the play of our life without knowing we have been playing it out the way we have. Now we are awake to our sleep. Now we are seeing from once blind. This is all that the word awakening is about. This is the tip of the iceberg, the skin deep, of where we are about to go.

What Are My Loops?

Everything I am experiencing, that disturbs, upsets, and triggers me is the past looping itself. Everything not loving to others and to myself, all my neurosis and insecurities, are there to be seen as potential opportunities of alchemy. All my impatience, my frustration, my worry, my scarcity, my scurry and hurry anxiety, all my self-doubts, my limiting beliefs, my self-critic, self-judge, my belittling mental chatter, and all my needs to soothe are all being presented.

It is also my constant unconscious looping of my resistance to what is, my reactions to how life is, my non-acceptance of what is, to how others are, my bitching, complaining, gossiping, blaming, criticizing, and wallowing.

I'm looping myself into myself, using and

wasting all my creative energy. I am not the author of my life; I'm following an old default script and nervous system patterning. And this is, in actuality, absolute futility and insanity. And this is a constant drain that I suffer, constricting myself, being a victim of my own unawareness. Literally most and much of how I am is me looping me into myself, moment to moment, cementing the same old same, again and again. I'm stuck in survival when I could be in creation. I'm perpetuating and stagnating when I could be regulating and in constant elevation.

I do not react to anything new. Nope. I'm re-acting my old act of me. I'm looping the blind script of my old actor who is unconscious and unaware of my self-inflicted constant reactions. I'm in my own moment to moment re-coding and downloading of the same codes and loops of me.

I'm literally a looping logarithm of me. I am my own feed, feeding myself my fodder and food of the same old same thoughts, feelings, narratives, and reactions, without anything new. I experience myself by being myself without any conscious awareness or changing the content of me. I disturb me, upset me, trigger me, worry me, frustrate me, and generally code download how I am.

So now I know much more about my old operating systems. Great. But this is simply intellectual education, mental masturbation, understanding, knowledge, and all its over-articulation that can come with it. This is the skin-deep version of breaking loops. The education has to become embodied. And this is where the courageous, determined, discipline comes in. We have to ingest and digest it, then utilize it, metabolize it, and actualize it in every moment of every moment, transforming and alchemizing, and then live the experience of life embodying and constantly strengthening this process and practice.

This work is a direct threat to our old constructed human ego, its identity, and all the suffering it loops, normally feeds off, and is addicted to. This all feels unsafe to the already default unsafe ethereal alarm systems set in place. And it will do anything it can to keep me kept where I am.

What would you be without upsets, triggers, disturbs, neurosis, insecurity, and the need to soothe, to escape to seek validations, gratifications, and satiations? You would be Free.

Using *The Map* and the *Operating Manual* and breaking loops is very much like living a whole new life after driving an automatic car for thirty years, and then being given a manual, stick shift, to operate for the first time. This is a new practice and process while also trying not to drive and live the old way. It's a constant clunky, fumbling, stumbling, slip, and get back on the horse.

You will be presented, like a spiral, your loops. If you don't break your loops the spiral brings them around again for you to face and feel and break. You are your own Fibonacci in creation. Breaking a loop does not mean the spiral won't bring them around again. You will be continually presented the loops until the lesson is truly learned and mastered. Mastery is not a half-ass, one-hit quick fix.

The student learns the teachings, mastering along the way, becoming the master, while always being the humble student to the mastery.

Default Setting

My nervous system, my survival mechanism, has been set to my childhood circumstances and environment and how I felt. I took on my parents' energy, tempers, anxieties, frustrations, impatience, and much else like an osmosis. I also had to perform to feel safe, to feel accepted, to keep parents happy. I had to perform to feel validated and safe, to keep teachers happy. And I was always trying to fit in with peers and comparing and competing within myself, with this constant performance pressure and anxiety. This becomes a varying degree of unsafe for all of us.

I was also over-stimulated with TV and all else out of nature, noisy and disturbing, in my home and family life. How much shouting and punishment, violence, and all else all contributed. To varying degrees, I got trapped in a mild to heavy survival mode, a fight-or-flight constant to keep up, feel safe, feel loved, perform, and keep others happy. My nervous system became far from regulated and normal. And yet it all seems normal. My little child is now operating in a specific unaware, unconscious, dysfunction of abandonment and a bucket load of neurotic, insecure, wounded, hurt and pain, performance pressure, and feeling unsafe trying to survive.

As an adult, I am stuck in this default setting, no matter what the outside brings to me. I will always return to the familiar of my body's survival dysfunction and dysregulation until I stop looping it and start regulating it.

It Takes a Village

This refers to the ideal natural human upbringing of our human history. A tribe, a community, a village of many adults and many children of all different ages all looked after each other, being there, supporting each other with zero to no pressure to perform or trying to feel safe. This is a constant of acceptance, approval, validation, attention, safety, and love. Take this all away, and we are now "void of the village" from day one.

Our parents struggle and frustrate, get impatient, and short tempered to varying degrees depending on their own inability to regulate their own nervous systems, their own emotions, their own childhood stuck inside them, their own loops.

Just telling a child to be quiet, at home, or out and about hits a nerve of the child. A child should be wild, noisy, and in nature. We take them out of their nature and try to make them be how we want. That alone is a pressure of having to be how others want. That feels unsafe to be us. That feels not good enough, just to be us. This means self-abandonment, again and again, to be who someone else demands.

Now we are simply, constantly dysregulated out of our nature, out of a village, struggling to feel good enough and safe, performing our mild to heavy anxious act.

Not OK is our nervous system default setting. We keep this feeling, keeping us seemingly safe in the familiar unsafe feelings of our coded, looped, downloads that are stuck in that ethereal operating mode.

The average adult human uses twenty percent of their lung capacity eighty percent of the time. We are literally in a mild to heavy dysregulated and anxious stress as a normal everyday operating system. This is our stuck fight or flight. This is a huge negative to our ability to do the work, to move through our unresolved issues as they are being presented moment to moment. We are operating much faster and more anxious than our potential. We operate at our default breathing and not our factory setting. We operate shallow and not deep and slow. We are simply far from regulated.

So, that's the quick understanding of the cause. We, how we are, how we operate, our neurosis and insecurities, are the effect. We now have a soup of suffering pains, hurts, labeled wounds, traumas, limiting beliefs, unresolved issues, and unmet needs that are all ruled by a wonderfully dysregulated nervous system. And it is all of these that keep looping again and again in our normal daily life as triggers, upsets, and disturbs.

And it is all of this that we can actually use, all our suffering pain, our neurosis and insecurity, our bag of unloved not good enough-ness, our darkness, our emotions and feelings, to in lighten, bit by bit, loop by loop, moment by moment. It's all being presented as opportunities to face, feel, and heal.

If I'm far from regulated, which most are, it's not easy to face the pain. We need a space to work in to break the loops.

Most are simply bypassing the pain by soothing it, escaping it, or over-compensating for it to try to change it. We have a thousand ways to not regulate, to not feel the pain, the dis-ease, the restlessness, the discomfort, the unease of life, the neurosis. Or we protect it and project and point and blame from it.

How We Soothe

We all soothe in many ways. We are soothing addicts. We have been doing so for most of our lives. We have never learned to just sit in the dis-ease, the unease, the discomfort, the restlessness, as well as the arising pain and hurt feelings. Life becomes a loop of avoiding feelings as well as soothing. Because we've always done so, we continue to do so. Because we have always felt the way we have inside of us, we have always tried to soothe it from outside of us. Because we have always felt unworthy, not good enough, unsafe, and unloved, we seek soothing outside of us. Because the pains and shame and guilt of our childhood call us, we soothe them instead of facing them, regulating them, feeling them, dissolving them, elevating from them, and healing them.

We are riddled with suffering on so many levels of what they label as abandonment wounds and traumas. I call it the unloved pain. It's calling us to face it and feel it. But we have never done this, never knew to do this. So, we do as we have always done; we escape, numb, distract, over-compensate, stimulate, sedate, snap, react, defend, and attack, as well as soothe. It's all soothing to a degree.

We Soothe With

Sugar, food, pills, porn, arousal, orgasm, chasing, dating, attention seeking, marriage, weed, booze, TV, social media, screens, noisy bars, clubs, rewards, satisfactions, excitements, shopping, stimulations, distractions, sedations, external validations, labels, and all that numbs and escapes, as well as over-compensations like success, status, and fame. Look at me, lack of me, I say.

Our deep lack, discomfort, unease, and suffering pain of the self seeks externally to soothe itself, to try to fill itself.

Excitement and satisfaction start at their highest points and then come down. Now you are caught in the kiss chase, rat race, hamster wheel of not enough-ness seeking for more. It's all external satiations, validations, instant gratifications, and stimulation addiction. This is far from internal salvation, elevation, regulation, and actual inner peace and contentment from within.

Most of us have never spent a moment sitting with ourselves without reaching, crutching, using, and soothing. It's just rampant and normalized. What's wrong with this? Well, we run from our inner dis-ease we don't want to sit with, face, and feel. So, now we ignore it, because we don't actually know it's asking to be faced, felt, regulated, and healed. It lives inside us calling us, constantly. This emotional dis-ease is not actually being eased, just soothed temporarily. It's being masked, smothered, veiled, and covered. We run and hide and seek constantly.

If we took the phones, TV, screens, dating apps, and substances away from most people, they would literally go stir crazy and feel totally unable to deal with the uprising of dysregulated discomfort and pain. This pain has been asking to be met our whole lives. This pain was never seen or met or heard by parents or schools or peers, and it now presents itself for us to do so. We kept pushing it all down, soothing it, again and again. And it kept looping back up to be faced and regulated.

We can't regulate from trying to escape.

We were constantly being told by parents and teachers, again and again. We never truly got to express our feelings or even feel comfortable or safe to do so. We had to be quiet. We had to behave. We had to be how others wanted us to be. We had to fit the narratives of how we should be. We were judged, criticized, scorned, told off, berated, belittled, smacked, given the silent treatment, given bad grades, and generally lived feeling quite unloved and unsafe for much of our childhood. Add this up, and you have a child full of pain, shame, and hurt, feeling unsafe, not good enough, unloved, stupid, bad, wrong, not important, etc. That's a lot of pain and emotion wanting to be loved. We simply stuffed it all down every time. Shame, guilt, pain, shame guilt pain, again and again. We had so much pressure to perform, so many hurts and pains, so much guilt and shame that it all seemed like normality. It was far from it. And it all got stuffed in and stuck.

No one was there for this pain, no one asked us about this pain, listened to this pain, or truly met this pain for where we were. No one even knew of this pain; we just hid it, didn't express it, even if asked, because we were too afraid to be so vulnerable. And so, we started to find any way we could to not face it. We played out our life feeling unloved, not good enough, unworthy, unsafe, always trying to not feel it, trying to soothe it, or overcompensate from the outside. It became the great pretend. It was also the constant of us abandoning us to simply feel safe and fit in and feel loved, feel validated, feel accepted, feel approved of. We over-compensated for our unloved pain; we soothed it again and again. And so, we abandoned our authentic self again and again.

Take it all away, the hide-and-seek, the distractions, the trying to get external validations, the instant soothing gratifications, the satiations, and we will simply feel a deep mountain of the unloved pain. And that's what we have to face and feel. That's what requires regulating.

There, that should express why you feel the way you do. Inside you are ten thousand wounds wallowing and hiding from being faced and felt. We soothe it, again and again, without knowing we should be meeting the pain, facing the pain, creating space for the pain, feeling the pain all the way through, and so allowing it to move and dissolve. This is the constant of regulating and resolving the dysregulation and unresolved.

If, as a child, our parents were regulated, able to manage their own triggers and pain, able to function free of their own dark and blind wounds, we might have far less to contend with as adults. If we had someone who always hugged us and loved us, even when we made a mistake, talked gentle to us, asked how we were feeling, instead of telling us how to feel, allowed us to express how we felt, and held a space for the mess of our young, innocent minds, we might have a greater degree of emotional regulation as adults. If there were no performance pressure, we might feel good enough, just for being us, we might feel OK within ourselves, safe.

No one did anything wrong. They simply did what they knew, not knowing they were totally unable to know any different. They now say a child up to a certain age can't truly cognitively know right and wrong. And so, every time frustration, impatience, short temper, or performance pressure was put onto us we simply interpret it, feel it, as we're not good enough, we're bad, wrong, unloved, and unsafe as we are, being us. We do this, we interpret, create emotions, perceptions, and beliefs about ourselves and others and live this make believe of pain and shame.

This constant adds up, loops, codes and downloads, and then gets stuck on repeat, like a broken record. This is all accompanied by the nervous system dysregulation and all the other systems in the body and mind that follow like a bad orchestra.

The mental, emotional, psychological, neurological, biological, physiological, chemical, ethereal self is now constructed from all this wounded hurt and pain. The human child and its very operating systems are caught within the constructs of itself; it all plays out as normality. We are now reacting and repeating loops on autopilot, default settings.

I never tell anyone to stop soothing. I myself have had a long journey through many habits and addictions. To soothe, to not face the pain, is normality. What I say is to start to breathe slowly and deeply. Maybe ask the pain, the restlessness, the discomfort what it feels, then breathe, regulate, sit with it, and be with it, no matter how tough it seems. Just try for fifteen minutes at first, before you soothe.

Say to the pain, "It's OK. I'm here. I got you."

This small amount of time, before wanting to soothe, is practice for being with the pain. Keep being aware; don't fall into a narrative. Maybe go for a walk in nature and keep breathing. It can feel excruciating, but you won't die. You are learning to sit and regulate what you normally avoid and soothe.

The nervous system is set in default dysfunction for survival. So it does not want you to function in regulation. This is the slow but sure re-set back to factory setting.

Soothing Is Not Healing

Feeling it all, all the way through its duration is how we regulate, grow, elevate, not rely, depend, and attach to habitual forms of escapes and sedations. Soothing is the antithesis of being able to naturally regulate, to just be at peace. We simply can't be with ourselves. It's virtually never done.

The more we get used to sitting in the pain, again and again, moving through it, the more we regulate and master our way to mastery. Being ruled by, and a slave to, is normal. We remain addicts to not facing our discomfort and soothing it.

This is determined, courageous, and disciplined work. Just don't pick up the phone and scroll. Just don't turn on the TV. Just don't stuff your face with sugar, turn on the porn, get on a dating app to get a fix of hits of validation, or anything to somehow change the feeling. Just sit with it, breathe slower and deeper than normal, not too harsh, feeling it all, and move through it.

Soothing tries to release the discomfort of the inner feeling. And that means we still keep the feeling, still stay in the constant of our deep-down pain we have never truly met, faced, and moved through. This is a journey to learn how not to hide, not to escape, not to numb, but to dissolve the old unresolved pain and regulate from within.

We are learning to reset our nervous system without using soothing. We are learning to bring ourselves back to a place that is always calm, not restless, not uneasy, not reaching, crutching, using, soothing.

Be still and know.

Regulate the Nervous System

A deer in the woods is eating food. It has a nervous system that has a regulated homeostasis, a normal factory setting. It wanders around quite calmly. Then it senses something, and its body becomes alert, ready, and floods itself with chemicals to assist in fight or flight. The deer can run away until safe or fight until safe. Either way the deer's body does what it does and eventually comes back to calm, to peace, to regulation, to factory setting. This is virtually the same for all creatures.

The human child, unfortunately, living in the stress and mess of the nuclear family and all its dysfunction of parental dysregulations, its constant performance pressure, is constantly trying to feel safe but never really rests and regulates to a truly calm place. To varying degrees each of us has set our survival mechanism to however we experienced our childhood. This is our dysfunction, dysregulation, default setting, we get stuck in.

In the normal nuclear family, we have the man go off to work. He is now absent in time. Unlike the village, now half our support system is not there. And due to the heritage of the indoctrination and conditionings of the patriarchy, the man is mostly emotionally absent even when he is there. This has a knock-on effect to the mother. She, now on her own, not with village support, goes into a survival mode and out of her nurture and nature. Again, to varying degrees, the child will now feel this via an energetic exchange, an osmosis, and regulate to a default survival mode and feel unsafe while trying to feel safe, to varying degrees. The child is now like a deer, always trying to mentally figure it out, void of a village, trying to feel safe, to survive, from a mild to heavy dysregulation, depending on the dysfunction and absence of one or two of the parents, in time and emotionally, as well as the atmosphere of their home life.

My mother was neurotic, erratic, loud, aggressive, reactive, impatient, angry, and violent. My stepfather was calm but was not at all emotionally involved. In fact, he was quite emotionless. He was simply cordial and had surface conversation with little emotional connection or safety. He was distant, not safe. He was the average man of the house, being the man, as sterile and normal as the man usually is. I never felt I could open up, trust, feel safe sharing how I felt about anything. When he did lose his temper, it was angry, loud, critical, and aggressive. My father was never really loud or violent to me. Yet he was full of violence and temper to others sometimes, which was always a delicate egg-shell environment, mildly scary to a degree. My stepmother was a very safe and sweet space. But I lived with my mom and stepdad ninety-eight percent of my time. I was terrified, frightened, and always on edge. The rules were very strict and constantly reinforced with cold sternness. School was a huge pressure. I was constantly ridiculed for not being to standard, not being an academic, and always felt lesser than for being the youngest child.

My anxiety, worry, impatience, temper, neurosis, insecurity, scarcity, and frustrations were all now deeply soaked in from where I lived and how I lived. My nervous system was a mess, and I was a messy stress inside my head. Soothing, escaping, and sedating in any way I could find became my way of life as I grew up. And all the deep unconscious anger and resentments all turned to violence. I was snap happy, trigger happy, reactional, and passive-aggressive. I was full of the pain of shame from being hurt, beaten, yanked around, restricted, confined, scorned, and screamed at. Sex, drugs, and rock and roll; self-harming; and hedonism became my soothing to try to somehow not feel all the pain, to escape myself, to regulate myself. Trying to get external validation and instant gratifications became my drugs.

We all have unknown aspects of our childhood ruling and fooling us. Our nervous system is kind of the captain of our ship. This starts to be dysregulated in the womb depending on our mother's own state of being. If our mother and father are fighting, we feel it. If our mother is anxious, we feel it. If our mother is worried, we feel it. This is the first formation of our nervous system.

If a child does not get held enough, screams, and is ignored, it's now flooding itself with stress chemicals and forming its nervous system for survival.

Then add the very stress and pressures of the nuclear patriarchal family to the varying degrees of its own dysfunction, and the society we live in, and we are operating in enough mess to have us constantly stuck in a mild to heavy fight or flight.

Our nervous system works in unison with the rest of our collective systems to create the resonance we keep resonating. We label these effects our neurosis and insecurities. These are a collection of self-inflicted self-repeated, self-scripted thoughts, feelings, perceptions, and beliefs we continually, perpetually repeat and react, loop and feel and think and believe and perceive from, resonating, repeating, verbalizing, self-criticizing, self-belittling, self-doubting, in negative self-talk, dysregulating, and generally creating a deeply unconscious re-coding downloading operating system. This software of us, this nervous system fight or flight, this neurological and emotional act we re-act is mostly a moment-to-moment unaware constant looping that feeds itself to keep itself fed and alive in its default survival.

Now we know why and how we operate. Now we have to regulate. We can have all the information and knowledge in the world, but if we don't actualize and embody and regulate our moments, our moments will simply keep repeating the loops and cementing the dysregulation, playing the same narratives, believing the same beliefs, and seeing life through these lenses of perceptions.

Breathe

As I've written, most people utilize twenty percent of their lung capacity eighty percent of the day. This means our captain, our nervous system, is mildly to heavily drunk at the wheel of our ability to remain at peace. To regulate, we must use our moments of not being regulated as potential and opportunities to become so.

Every moment I am not speaking, I have now trained myself to breathe slower and deeper than normal, much of the time, constantly regulating. Nothing too extreme but simply breathing through my nose, into my belly, then into my chest, then out my nose. The more I do this, the easier it becomes to remember, to inhabit and alter a lifetime of shallow breathing.

You have spent your whole life not conscious, not regulated. Your nervous system wants to keep you in that familiar survival.

As I started my new practice, I stuck notes in the car, on the mirror, on my laptop, and on other places saying "Breathe!" I was astounded at how I kept forgetting. My nervous system was doing its job, keeping me snapped right back to my default setting.

My factory setting should be conscious, aware, yet calm, at ease, at peace, like the deer eating in the woods, not neurotic or insecure, unsafe, in need, trying, searching, soothing, chasing, etc.

By regulating the moments of my normal dysregulation, my shallow breathing, by deeper, slower breathing, I am now slowing down within myself. This creates space. And space is essential for breaking loops. If there is no space, I remain unconscious and unaware, and I fall from grace and into my loops very quickly, like on autopilot.

I need to regulate to create the space, which in its very being, creates the strength of my conscious awareness muscle.

From the ability to learn to regulate and breathe, I am now in a greater position to catch my unconscious reactions, stop myself from falling into and attaching to thoughts and feelings, pointing, blaming, and narrating or looping my neurosis and insecurities.

Falling Unconscious

Let's say my shallow breathing and dysregulation have me standing on the edge of a cliff, inside me. And every time I get anxious, frustrated, worried, impatient, in scarcity, or any other triggered reaction, neurosis, or insecurity, I fall off the edge; I fall unconscious and then straight into my loops. If I start to breathe, calm down, slow down, create space, that space backs me away from the edge. And the more space I have, the more space I can operate in and maneuver to break my loops or do my inner child work. Because if and when something arises or happens, I am now further away from falling off the edge of my inner cliff, my unconsciousness. I create the space to become strengthened in my conscious awareness to then be able to do the work.

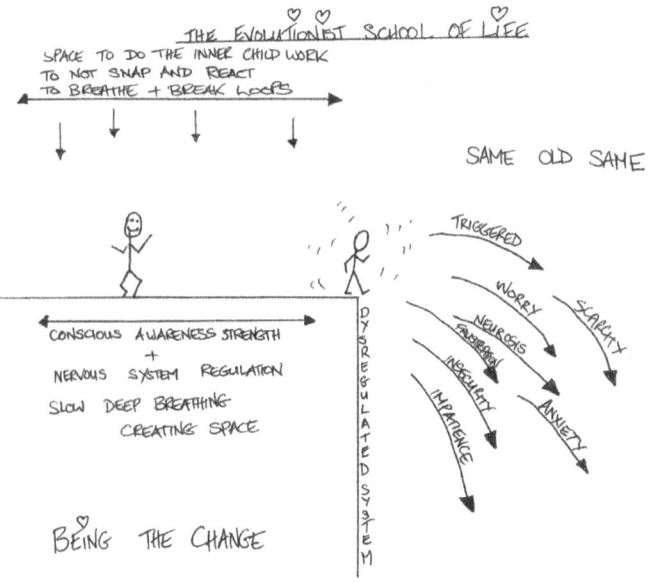

Breathe! Slowly, deeply, with awareness. This can be done in virtually every moment of life unless we are talking. There is no excuse but your excuses. We are a habit and addict to the biological need to feel and stay dysregulated. It is all a chemically enhanced addiction. The body will flood itself constantly in fear, insecurity, and neurosis to keep itself kept in the familiar default.

If we are constantly in fight or flight, our immune system is constantly compromised. The gut and much else will be affected by our restless, anxious dis-ease of dysregulation.

Breath, in ancient translations, comes from the word *spirit*. They are entwined in each other. The more dysregulated you feel, the less breath, the less conscious, the more we suffer our mindless neurosis. The more we learn to return to breath, become a walking living regulation meditation, the more we regulate to create space to elevate, to resonate and in lighten. This means we learn to live and move out of our head and be more in our heart.

Spirituality is just a label, and a fad label of today. In actuality and truth, it's simply about becoming more consciously aware to the degree that we don't get caught in our mindlessness, our darkness, anymore. We become the space of our conscious awareness, not the mess we normally attach to and fall into. We are learning to be of spirit and space and not of the ego mind and all its attachments, identifications, and madness.

Become a Breathing Living Regulation Meditation

Breath and Triggers and Upsets

So, I am now learning to become aware, to consciously breathe, to slow myself down, to regulate, to practice this process. This is me creating space. This is now the basis for my living meditation regulation. From this, I strengthen the muscle of my conscious awareness as well as regulating my nervous system. I am consciously breathing as I type this.

Stage one is now in operation. This is a discipline. Remember, you have been unaware and unconscious in breaking loops, in regulating, in breath, your whole life.

With this space, I now become that much more vigilant, aware, and conscious. I'm also aware of how easily I fall from grace and back down into the lower dimensions of unconscious unawareness and into my reactivity and the victim mentality and narratives of this blindness. I call it blindness from the biblical statement, "Once was blind and now I can see." We are clearing the lenses of our perceptions, moment by moment, to in lighten the self into clarity.

Most of my life I was totally blind to how I am now. I was never aware, always falling into my darkness, my dysfunction and dysregulation, feeding it with my loops of neurosis and insecurity. All my limiting beliefs, my bag of unloved not-good-enough-ness, simply played out as if it were who I was, how I operated, who I believed and perceived myself to be. I had perfected this blindness my whole life. I was an addictive habit of me. I operated that software without any conscious control or authorship. I was on autopilot default settings.

My subconscious, neurological pathways, and nervous system all worked in unison to keep the patterns, loops, and reactions looping their patterns and reactions. I was a loopy software program of me. And these all released chemicals into my blood that became a familiar factory of addictive and familiar feelings.

So, now I keep remembering to breathe, creating more space. And now I am also in the understanding that I am the creator of my loops, and so I can also be the one who breaks my loops.

Here is a list of what actually loops within my unconscious unawareness, feeding my nervous system:

Worry, scarcity, impatience, frustration, anxiety, insecurity, self-doubt, self-critic, self-judge, limiting beliefs of not feeling good enough, feeling unloved, feeling unsafe, feeling stupid, wrong, bad, unworthy, undeserving, guilt, resentment, and a boatload of shame that lives behind much of my negative self-talk, reactions and my emotional dysregulations.

We loop this soup of suffering without knowing we are the chef. We keep creating loops without knowing we can break them.

Now I have my shopping list of loops. Now I'm intellectually educated, in the understanding of.

Now I have more knowledge, and as written in *The Map*, all is now my experience and my responsibility.

Intellectual understanding is mute and void if we don't embody and actualize it into the moment-to-moment experience of life, of our actuality of our ethereal, emotional self. That's just the spiritual bubblegum I love to joke about.

Intellectualized information and knowledge are the spiritual ego's favorite food to ingest and mentally masturbate with. It's an addiction to seeking temporary trauma hacks. The mental can't ever do the work of the experience, the embodiment, of the ethereal alchemy of actualizing each moment of every moment. The mind stuffs itself to try to get more information, more knowledge.

I know.

I now have an understanding.

It all makes sense.

This is the intellect.

Courses, classes, retreats, plant medicines, podcasts, weekly sessions of coaching and therapy, yoga, kundalini, breath classes, sound baths, the gym, and all else that are ingested and acted out are a multibillion-dollar industry of stuffing it in at a surface level, getting quick intellectual fixes or part-time releases and regulations, and then negating ninety-five percent of the moment to moment of the looping of life. If you are truly operating your moments, breaking loops, you will feel zero need for anything else. Because a need to comes from a lack of. And that is a loop of lack to feel and face. It's that genius.

You can't stuff a turkey and then expect the stuffing to cook it.

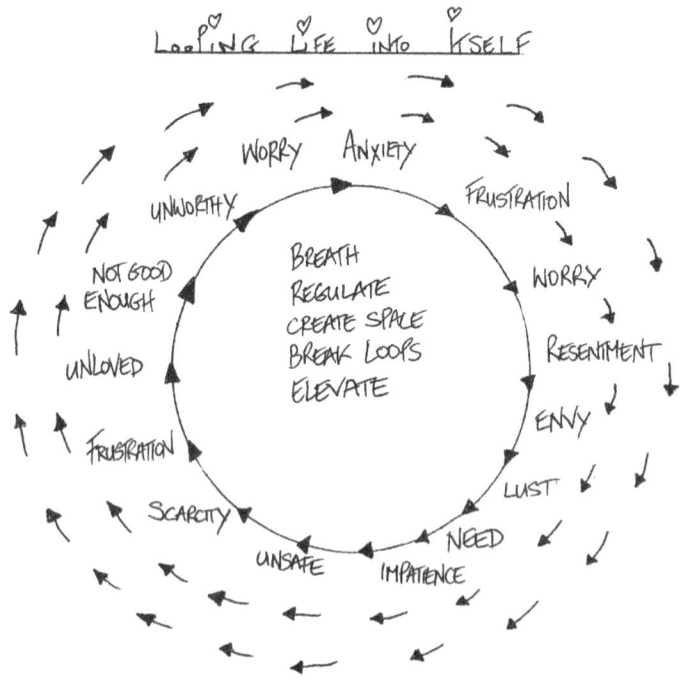

The Next Stage

We have now become an educated, conscious breather in the making. If we find the courage, discipline, and awareness, we can be in this constant practice and process. Be patient, have compassion for the process and journey. Let's take the greatest and most obvious emotional loop most people constantly suffer from, even if they have more than enough.

Scarcity

We were raised with people who mostly repeated, complained, spoke of, worried about, made comments of, berated us about, maybe guilted us, screamed at us, got frustrated, got anxious, got impatient because of, and were perpetually dysregulated by all these attributes and effects of the subject around money. This was a resonating ener-getic for most of us about scarcity, one of the many labels of the poverty of our being. These constant hypnotic suggestions, from home and the media programming, as well as much else of friction, ten-sion, and dysfunction, became the formulation of one major aspect of our operating systems. We con-stantly swam in the soup of our parents' neurotic energy, their survival fight-or-flight nervous system of inner poverty and the script we soaked up.

Fast-forward, and now we are adult clones repeating the same dialogue to ourselves, and even to our own children. The neurotic and unconscious rampant, insecurity of our inner poverty, our scar-city, rules and fools us, looping itself into itself. And our nervous system is totally operating in this default programming and conditioning. This is the resonation of dysregulation and a narrative to drive it into a victim story.

Most who have money come from what they call new money. They were still raised in scarcity. And old money, which is many generations of wealth, live without a bone of poverty. The rich stay rich, and the poor stay poor. And many who have made new material wealth don't keep it in their future generations, because they hand down the sabotage of their inner poverty, their scarcity.

Being raised in a middle-class family with a nice home and knowing we were reasonably comfortable, compared to friends and their backgrounds, meant nothing. The amount of strict rules about lights being left on, the screams and shouts and guilt for how much things cost, for how much school costs, for every aspect of life, was a constant unsafe fear. The pressure to be something, to be a success, to work hard, to become more, to get and attain security with money was in actuality a conditioning of insecurity all by itself.

Later in life, I found myself riddled with scarcity, doubt, and fear for the future, even with plenty of money, mild fame, and much flowing in. It was never enough. I was never enough. This was a huge undertaking to break. I always stayed at a certain level of inner poverty, which always remained regardless of what I attained. This was a huge part of breaking my loops.

So, we are now consciously breathing, creating space.

Usually, scarcity just happens, loops itself, re-codes its download, continues, subsides, loops, continues, feeds itself, and so on. We simply feel a feeling, go to the mental narrative and neurosis, the neural pathways, and play it all out without even thinking about it. We perpetuate the state of scarcity by stating it in our feelings, our dysregulations, our emotions, and our inner narrations, and words we speak.

We resonate our poverty mind, thoughts, words, and feelings, in the body. It's old ghosts from our childhood haunting us again and again without any awareness and with no ghost buster in sight. Something outside us can trigger it, or the inside feeling or thought just decides to feed us some scarcity chemicals and cause a chain reaction of nervous system dysregulations to stay in the familiar unsafe feeling.

The familiar now keeps looping and feeding itself loops of scarcity. The body and mind require us to keep it fed with the same old same. So, it keeps doing so. Scarcity riddles most people for much of their moments and much of their life. It's the tune and resonance of fear and poverty.

We all have our own unique basket of varying degrees of loops to break. And scarcity rules a massive percentage of the human population.

Example
Here Comes a Bill!

Straightaway, my body and mind are kicking into a full nervous systems alert and are ready to flood me with scarcity feelings and thoughts. This is the tsunami force, the gravitational pull of the loops. In an instant, I can go from relative peace to financial panic. This can happen when the car warning light goes on, a tire goes flat, the dog gets sick and has to go to the vet, a business deal falls apart, or any circumstance where I have to spend money where I didn't plan or want to. The potentials for triggering the internal poverty from our childhood are endless. Look at all I wrote. Bill, car, tire, dog, business, etc. All are happenings that happen. They are life being life. Life tends to do that. It has events and situations and circumstances. How I am, how I react, how I fall from grace, fall off the cliff, fall into the loops of scarcity and feed it, are all my choices, my creations. I unconsciously attach to my feelings and narratives into a familiar loop. This keeps and feeds the whole system being the same old same, again and again.

Change the Same Old Same

The bill arrives. Scarcity starts to be felt, then the mind kicks in. Now I am already in the loop in a split second. If I am consciously aware, have created space, I can catch it, detach from it, break it before it closes. Normally, the feeling and narrative simply default into their autopilot, and the chain reaction floods me intoxicated and unconscious with scarcity. Now I am blindly in the loop, looping away, and my nervous system kicks into survival, and my mind dribbles along with the normal panic, fear, doubts, and worry scurry or neurotic self-suffering narratives and anxiety. Yes, we do this to us. Not the external, not our circumstances. Many wealthy people also suffer scarcity. It's their karmic work. It's their childhood stuck stuff. It's their nervous system playing out its addiction to the familiar default survival. Many over-compensate for their poverty within by striving to gain external validations, to be successful. Then they simply meet their deep unconsciousness of scarcity soon enough, in the mirror of life. Their nervous system does not know material wealth, external validations.

So that's the looping of normality just constant as constant is, moment to moment, day by day, God knows how many times. We are experts at being in scarcity, a perfected malpractice.

What many don't realize is that they keep sabotaging their financial life by being in scarcity because the nervous system is keeping us in the familiar to survive. To become content, have no scarcity, be full and filled and wealthy within, is not familiar. So, we unknowingly, unconsciously, make sure we don't step out of this normal operating space. The ruler rules and fools us to remain in our poverty, our lack. And we have been doing this our whole life. We inhabited our neurosis and insecurity, our nervous system's default, to perfection. And for most of us, life will simply mirror our inner world right back.

Many even resent people with money or success. They curse, envy, have jealousy, and ridicule. These people are literally saying they don't want money. That's how powerful we are in our creations. They hate the very thing they want.

Breaking the Loop

L et's do this in a breakdown of slow motion. (This all happens in a split second. This is why regulating and creating conscious awareness space is so important.)

Something is triggered from inside or seemingly from the outside.

You feel the feeling in an instant.

Breathe deeper and slower from your nose into your belly and then the chest and out the nose.

Become the awareness.

Don't be ruled and fooled by the nervous system.

Watch the mind.

Don't attach to the scarcity narrative that tries to grab you.

Detach, observe, and keep breathing.

Be the awareness.

Feel the tsunami, the neurotic, energetic, gravitational pull of scarcity trying to pull you down and in.

See it, know it, watch it, BREATHE.

Know it as an old pattern.

Breathe.

Stay the watcher. Stay aware. Remain conscious.

Sit with it.

Face it.

Feel it, feel the pain, the fear.

Don't believe or attach to the narrative that the mind is trying to pull you into.

The loop wants to grab you in.

The loop wants to close and then keep you looping in it.

This is the emotional ethereal energy of our past wanting to close itself into itself.

Just feel the pain, the pull, the old pattern, the old you trying to close the loop.

Sit in it, feel it, expand and shine the light of awareness onto it.

This is the most powerful and sometimes deeply excruciating part. It's like the old pattern and program addict is in a tantrum to try to get you to fall into the loop, over the cliff, and then feed you the chemicals, get you to mindlessly become a victim and become the scarcity, the dysregulation, and feed all your old operating systems. You will feel it, sense it, listen to it trying to narrate and dysregulate you. The power of our consciousness is key.

Remain the light of awareness.

Breathe.

Keep breathing.

Watch it, sit with it, be with the discomfort; it should start to dissolve in power. Hold your place and space. Hold your attention and awareness and keep breathing. Let the feeling happen. It will eventually move through its duration and reduce in force. Don't break your awareness. Don't stop your conscious observations. Keep breathing. Stay all the way through the breaking of the loop. This is courageous, determined, and very disciplined work. You are learning to burn through what you never have done before. This is the road through our hell to get to our heaven.

As it weakens, stay strong. Don't give up your detached awareness. Keep breathing. When it's been a spacious expansion for a while, free of narrative or any pull, you can reassure yourself that you are now elevated and not the old story. Now you can add some worthy wealth and abundance of gratitude feelings into the space.

Now you have learned the process of breaking loops. I like to say thank-you to myself, again and again, for the great work. This is one of many more of the same loops to come. This is about gaining conscious awareness strength, regulating when we normally do the antithesis. This is a practice and process. This is not one event and done. This is an old habitual life of looping now turning to breaking loops. The more we catch the loops and break the loops, the more we master and become stronger in conscious control. The more we do this, the more we regulate our nervous system.

Scarcity will try to grab you again and again and again. The old nervous system will continue to stay in survival as it has done your whole life until you regulate it and train it otherwise.

We are working toward a whole new operating system. Be patient and have compassion for where you are. It's OK. It's always OK, wherever you are. You just feel it's not OK, think and narrate it's not.

Scarcity is a very powerful constant for most, for most of their lives. It seems reckless to not have money worries, to not be overcautious, to not be frugal, to not be anxious about the bills and all else financial. You can be financially smart and responsible without the neurosis and its vice grip. It allows the flow of life to flow and actually open us up to receive more.

Example

If you are going to go out and have a meal at a nice restaurant and scarcity comes up, watch it, see it, feel it, don't attach a narrative to it, be with it, and move through it. If it comes up when you see the menu, see it, feel it, move through it, breathe, and don't narrate. When the bill comes, be ready to not fall off the cliff. This is not being negligent. This is enjoying your choices and not ruining them with neurosis and loops. This simple meal can become a perfect experience of breaking the loops, regulating your nervous system. A scarcity-free meal.

This was the effect of educate, regulate, elevate, and resonate. After we break the loop, we expand and elevate above the consciousness that would have looped and had us spinning downwardly into our lack. We have regulated where we would have done the opposite. And we now resonate at a whole new space and place within. We literally in lighten ourselves compared to the weight and darkness of the past looping.

Don't let down your guard. This is about always becoming vigilant, aware, and conscious to the ego's smarts to feed itself old patterns and ways. Suffering is the ego's favorite food.

Becoming aware, breathing, and creating space are key to breaking loops. If we have not practiced breathing, the force will drag us very quickly into the unconscious loop because we are on the edge of the cliff inside.

We can also add a little inner child work to this. Each of these loops are old stories, old patterns.

I say to myself, "This is an old story. We're not living this anymore. This is not who we are. I got you. It's OK. You're safe. It's OK." Breathe.

These words are always calming and reassuring. These are what most of us required about life and money as a child, instead of the hypnosis of our parents' looping neurosis and scarcity.

The most empowering thing we need to hear and wanted to hear as a child and got the opposite, was "It's OK."

We can apply this same phrase, principle, and practice with all our neurosis and insecurity.

This example can be applied to frustration, to impatience, to anxiety, to worry.

It's astounding how we replay our broken record of emotional loops, belittling, critical, judgments, moment to moment, with no realization. It's our blind bleeding beggar of our abandonment constantly being the same old same.

"It's OK. I'm here. I've got you."

This mantra, and breathing, can be used to bring us back from many of life's emotional and mental suffering loops.

The medicine for the dis-ease is the moment.

Elevating

We learn to breathe. We start to practice breaking loops of this and that, of all that we unconsciously plague ourselves with. We start to strengthen a lifetime of unconscious unawareness as we start to move along life and life keeps presenting us opportunities. We keep in lightening, to start to respond and not react, to expand and not contract. We are now far more conscious, far more aware, and we expand and elevate within ourselves. We are now facing and feeling far more than before, instead of falling into them and attaching a narrative and looping the loops closed.

One very important note:

Be compassionate and gentle on this journey. You have been blind to this way of seeing and perceiving your whole life, and it will be a stumbling, fumbling travel before it starts to truly become second nature. When you catch yourself, after you have reacted, fallen blind, don't berate yourself, beat yourself up, belittle yourself, judge yourself, criticize yourself. That's just adding more shame and blindness to your bump in the darkness, creating more victim to your low down. The very fact that you saw that you reacted, saw you were looping, means you are consciously aware of your unconscious unawareness. That is part of the process. You still managed to see through your trip and stumble. That deserves a gift of grace to yourself, not a scorn and put-down. This is how genius it is. You can't make a mistake or fail. You can simply always learn to see a clearer way, every time, bit by bit, step by step. There is no right or wrong, just where you are doing the best you can. And this must be seen for others and where they are. If I don't break the loop straightaway and I fall a little unconscious and then realize, I always say to myself, "It's OK. It's OK." Where I am is always OK.

Events, Situations, Circumstances, and Other People

L ife seemingly consists of all of these labels. And yet, it's not actually true. All is as it is. All happens how it happens. How I am, how I react or respond, how upset and triggered I get, is how I allow myself to be, how I decide to be, how I experience my life, how I fall into my loops, or not.

The mastery of life, of the self, is the full and utter responsibility and accountability for our own experiences. And this is the deepest and most humble of wisdom to live by. When we know ourselves, know it is just us in here; we know we are ruling ourselves, and we live in the mastery. If not, we are mostly being fooled by our own blind unconsciousness, pushed around by seemingly external events, situations, circumstances, and other people and how they are. We live in slavery.

No one else pushes my buttons. I am the buttons, and I am the one who keeps pushing them.

Everything that ever happened in our life does not exist now. How I am about then, the past, is how I operate now, is how I decide and choose to be, knowingly or not, moment to moment. Everything that could and can happen in what we label as the future does not exist. But how I am about it is how I operate now. Now, what is happening in life, inside me, how I operate, how I feel, how I think, is me, doing it to me, consciously aware or not. I actually always have a choice to breathe, to regulate, to break loops, do inner child work, even if I don't know I do.

Everything is. That's that. That's the stark actuality of life. That's the what is of "It is what it is."

How I am about life, events, circumstances, situations, and others is all that there is. That is my very own perceived and believed, authored, and created personal reality.

I take accountability and responsibility for my thoughts, feelings, and emotions, or not.

Everyone else is where they are, to varying degrees, in their own blindness to this fact. And where they are, how they are, has nothing to do with me. We have to see this, and know this, and truly own this to be able to live this mastery of the self.

When circumstances, events, and situations happen, we react. We have a re-action within us. We go to a narrative and feeling within an instant and get anxious, frustrated, and impatient and start to worry, go to scarcity, feel shame, feel unloved, feel unsafe, and much more.

We are on autopilot, repeating and reacting the same re-act of our looping actor and wounded inner child. Breathe. The trigger is the ammunition inside, the lesson to learn, and the teacher is the mirror showing us to us. We have to create space to not fall into the loop, the pain, the mental chatter, the feelings, and get lost and blind.

Once was blind, now I can see. Once was lost, now I am found.

It is me, in here, learning to find myself, to see myself, to catch myself, and move through the lessons.

Something happens.

I breathe.

I observe myself.

I become the space of my conscious awareness.

I see the narrative trying to narrate.

My victim tries to pull me in.

I see it.

I don't attach to the narrative.

I sit with it and through it.

I break the loop.

Something happened. It was how it was. I am how I decide to be.

Other People

We live surrounded by others, by teachers in the school of life. They are all showing us our homework, mirrors showing us to us, showing us our deeply buried stuff, our hurt, our pain, our shame.

"If you think you are enlightened, go spend a week with your family," Ram Dass said.

How I am is mine. How others are is theirs.

Others point and project onto the screen of life their inner stuff in their words and actions or inactions. They are pointing from a place inside them.

What they say is about them, from them.

How they are about my words, how they feel, is about them.

How I am about their words is about me, from within me.

How I feel is about me.

And what I say is about me, from within me.

We all speak and react from how we are within us, from the lenses of our unresolved issues and our past pain and their perceptions.

I believe and perceive through me and speak through me, from me, about me. So do you. I only feel my own hurt and pain and then point and blame from it.

If I feel I have to snap, react, defend, and attack, raise my voice, be passive-aggressive, it's covering my old hurt, pain, and shame, protecting old feelings I don't want to face. This is what I feel in an instant before I react and send out my words.

My reactions are showing me to me, for me to break the loops of the feelings being mirrored back to me, triggered from inside me, so that eventually, as I practice and process, my system regulates and elevates and does not re-act my blind act, does not point outside of me, project, criticize, judge and blame, because I have dissolved and reduced the old hurt, pain, and shame. I empty the gun of me, of my ammunition.

Having a lot of social media presence has in the past caused great work for me to face on my old limiting beliefs and unresolved issues. I get insane amounts of projections, criticisms, judgments, and a general army and slew of blind attacks. I have witnessed how this feels inside me. It's like inviting thousands of strangers into your life to tell you how they think you should be.

So many parents and ex-girlfriends.

Being told was my trigger, for sure, as a kid. No one ever asked me how I felt. Everyone thought they knew what was best for me. They didn't. They never wanted to listen to me, meet me, or see me for where I was. They simply did what they did, from them, from where they were. But I felt like I was stupid, not good enough, bad, or wrong. Teachers, parents, religious teachers all did the same.

Fast-forward, and I meet the perfect partner who plays out the very same behaviors, and all my deep, unworthy shame reappears. I shut down, resent, and get angry. This was the perfect orchestration, perfect attract and match, to show me to me, show me to my lack.

So, I learned to face myself again and again and learn to bring love to my unresolved issues, my unmet needs, my limiting beliefs, all my shame. And then social media begins to test me, again and again, with these wonderful teachers in the mirror. I feel the shame and sit in it, with it, and allow it, knowing it's not them, their words, their criticisms, just my old hurt and pain. This was an amazing constant of teachers and lessons.

I had huge amounts of shame growing up. My teacher ridiculed me in front of my class, called me stupid and a ton more. That class then spread the word around the school. I was getting it from everywhere. Suicide was already on my mind constantly from my childhood and home life. This ridicule was excruciating. So, I became a tough guy to slam anyone who made fun of me. That stopped it quick enough. But the shame lived under all my charm and bravado, as with many men. That is the over-compensation to not face the feelings. This shame is what got triggered by life and others. This was my huge work to face and feel again and again.

How We Are with Others

Something happens or is said.

I'm triggered, upset, disturbed.

I feel a feeling I don't like.

I protect this feeling.

I react.

I create a narrative.

I point and project from my pain.

I blame, criticize, defend, attack, judge, or complain.

Or I just wallow in the shame and pain.

I am now a victim of not seeing the opportunity to face and feel my pain.

This all happens in an instant.

This is why breathing is so important to create space to not fall off the edge of the cliff and into the victim and its blind pointing projections. Instead, we feel the pain, face it, do inner child work, ask the feeling how it feels, see it's an old story, an old feeling, and sit and watch it, feel it, all the way through its duration and observe it dissolving. Again and again, I get to face my pain. And again and again I get to regulate, dissolve, elevate, and evolve. If I can't do the inner child work, I just sit and breathe and feel it and not attach to it, all the way, breaking the loop. This is the process of moment to moment. There is no destination, just a lighter life of more peace and more mastery, a constant of regulation, elevation, and evolving.

I am a masterpiece. I am the mastery to my peace.

No one disrespects me, insults me, or offends me. I feel disrespected, I feel insulted, I feel offended. They are descriptions of feelings. I feel unworthy, I feel unloved, I feel unsafe, I feel not good enough, I feel stupid, bad, wrong, etc. I FEEL. The feelings are inside, triggered inside, from long ago. Even these are just descriptions. Mostly, we feel the pain of what is labeled as shame. Much is a shame game. If you had no childhood shame, no ten thousand wounds, you would not feel the pain and hurt reflected back to you by others and their words or deeds. You would simply know that their words or deeds were all about them, their own hurt, pain, and shame that they didn't want to feel or face, so they point from it, project from it, and direct it at you, or others. When we know this, we can then find compassion for others and their unknown pain.

Example

A while ago, I saw a text message on a friend's phone from someone else to them, from someone in my past. It said that I did this and I did that. I was painted as quite the villain. It could have sent me into a shame-fueled rage and victim narrative, reacting, defending, attacking, feeling like I was being lied about, feeling disrespected.

That was how I used to be. I had not even contacted this person for well over a year. I had done much work on my shame since. Their words were all from them and all about them, where they were consciously. The circumstance being texted about was from nearly two years ago. I simply saw it for what it was. And there was no shame left inside me to get triggered. This very specific teacher in the mirror had given me a wonderful last test. They were texting and projecting to the other person their pain, their hurt. They were showing me this. And much of our pain and hurt come from feeling unloved, not good enough, and unsafe, still alive, long after the circumstances, and mostly from the actual inception point of childhood. That is how we carry our victim story and not face our pain. This is how we create others as the villain in our criticisms and blames. I didn't react, saw it as their old hurt, and came to compassion, even though what was being written about me was quite harsh. Theirs was theirs. Nothing to do with me.

Water under the bridge for some can still be a white-water rafting for others due to their own deep hurt. And that deep hurt is the feelings of pain of the unloved child being mirrored back to them, looping.

Example

A man drives his car fast and jumps a red light and then cuts in front on me. I slam on my breaks. He races off into the distance. A while ago I would have maybe raced along, leaned on my horn, screamed much foul loud language, and retold the story again and again all week long. "He did this to me. He this. He that." Me playing the victim.

That was then.

As he first appeared and I slammed on my breaks, I went straight to breathing. I slowed down and felt the feeling. I didn't fall into a loop, and I didn't go to a narrative. I had created space. And in this space, not on the edge of the cliff, I then found compassion for whatever was causing him to drive at such speeds. Who knows, maybe someone was in hospital. Maybe he was very late. Either way, he was driving as he was. That was that. How I reacted, or could have reacted, was about me. The old me would have felt disrespected. I would have felt like he treated me like an idiot. I would have felt stupid. I would have felt my old shame. But I was well regulated, and my shame was now quite diminished. It all dissolved in its moment.

Example

Someone I have known for a long time throws criticisms and labels at me. I hold a different opinion to the genocide played out by a dark ideology, regime, and government in the Middle East. They don't care to calmly, openly discuss; they simply throw angry words to attack me. My old self would have reacted, then fired back and got into an endless war of words, an ego battle of who's wrong and who's right.

He was utterly right from where he perceived, from his identifications of his beliefs and their indoctrinations. I felt a mild feeling, I observed it, didn't attach to a narrative, and simply breathed and didn't respond. I sat in the feeling and faced whatever it was. Maybe he felt belittled, or small, or stupid, or shame, because his beliefs felt threatened and unsafe. That's why most snap, react, and attack with defensive passive-aggressiveness. The ego has to be right. And if it does not want to reason, to see any other potential way, it simply covers its fragile identity, its deep shame, with angry snap reactions and projections. I watched myself come to compassion very quickly. The old me used to feel shame, would feel attacked, would snap, react, become defensive from my own hurt ego, feel like no one listens, feel stupid, feel deep shame, and do the same as them and throw labels their way. Now,

I was regulated and had done much work on my shame, so saw it all for what it was, not mine.

If I snap, react, defend, and attack or get passive-aggressive with words, it's my shame I don't want to face.

Many men are riddled with shame. This is their greatest hurdle to face and feel and not react from. That's the humble and vulnerable hero.

Theirs is theirs, mine is mine, and it is only an ego that gets entwined.

Realtionships
and Parents

Others show us to us. That's it.

A love relationship is the ultimate vehicle for what they label as healing, growth, for breaking loops, for conscious evolution, regulation, and elevation. It is the greatest mirror.

When we start to regulate, understand the map, the operating manual, we can start to express how we feel. Expressing and owning, taking full accountability and responsibility for our feelings is not the same as pointing, blaming, criticizing, judging, and saying, "You make me feel or that makes me feel."

No one makes you feel. Expressing is not reactional. Expressing is a regulated, vulnerable opening of what we feel, how we feel, without protecting, pointing, blaming, and projecting. Expressing is a deep intimacy of sharing our feelings and not hiding them or protecting them.

The mirror shows you to you, your hurt, your shame, your fear and pain you never faced and moved through since childhood. That's the genius. The more we regulate, create space, strengthen our conscious awareness, the more we are able to break the loops of our hurt child inside, our old code download patterns, and bring safety back to our nervous system. And the more we do this, the clearer we become. And then we start to see how nothing is about us. Much and most of what others say in relationships pointed at us is about the other person. What I feel, how I am, is all about me. This is the constant of compassion. I can have compassion and at the same time express how I feel.

"I'm feeling triggered."

"This is how I am feeling. This is what I'm expressing."

"How do you feel?"

Let them repeat what they think you said.

Now we are both relating and expressing and understanding on the same page.

There is this great technique of asking your partner if they have time to listen. They are now being primed to be aware and conscious. If they are ready, they can say yes or create a time soon in the day to sit and talk. You can also say that what you are about to express could trigger them. Now they are very aware compared to just one person unconsciously reacting, spewing, pointing, and projecting hurt feelings and words. This is a slowing down of the communication. This assists in creating a regulated space to process whatever is going to be expressed. This allows two people to be fully accountable and responsible.

We have a fear of the loss of love from our childhood, from a constant of not expressing our feelings, so we don't speak up. We then became people pleasers. Most of us do this, abandon ourselves again and again from this fear of what others will think or say. So, we shut up to feel safe. We have to be able to express and not fear.

The deep fear of the loss of love comes from a deep feeling of being unloved.

Once, in the past, someone I knew was quite aggressive in their delivery. Instead of criticizing or reacting, I asked if they would be willing to hear something I would like to express. They agreed. Now we created a container to meet each other. I simply expressed and asked if they could be a little gentle when they communicated with me. There was a pause. They then said they agreed and actually admitted that they could be a little obnoxious. And then they thanked me for expressing my feelings. I never used any words of judgment, blame, or attack. This could have been a war of words, projections, accusations, and criticisms, but it was a communication of expressing and meeting each other and resolving and evolving without conflict.

There is an amazing book about how to navigate and translate and communicate consciously and vulnerably. It should only be read by both people in a relationship who are regulated and willing. I expressed this in my book *The Map*.

Getting the Love You Want, by Harville Hendrix and his wife, Helen LaKelly. It's a truly humbling read.

A relationship is designed to mirror back and bring to the surface all your old stuff. They show you to you, and you show them to them. I feel my stuff, from within me, and they feel their stuff from within them. We are both there to hold a space, an unconditional container, to allow each other to express, and face our own issues. This is the deepest form of relating.

Being regulated is imperative to create space. Most people fall off the edge of their inner cliff constantly in relationships. That's how much work we are both being presented with.

All the unmet needs, limiting beliefs, and unresolved issues are going to rise to the surface, again and again, until we face them and feel our way through them, again and again.

What is triggered is mine to face, not fling it in the face of my partner in blame, criticism, judgment, and complaints. This goes for the both of us. We are a safe space for each other to be there for each other so we can do our own work.

What Gets Triggered in Relationships

Feelings of being unsafe, unloved, unworthy, not good enough, bad, stupid, unimportant, shame, fear and guilt are what are triggered from within us. We relate through these lenses of perception. So, these are what come to the surface to be worked on.

When we snap, react, defend, and attack, we are already falling off the edge of the cliff and projecting from our unsafe pain, hurt, and shame. We are now looping and bickering, caught in a pattern. This is nothing but two people protecting their pain, not expressing from it, and blaming each other with zero responsibility or regulation.

We meet and match at the same degree of our wounding, our pain, our dysfunction, our dysregulation. A deeply unloved, unsafe, unworthy person, dysregulated will meet someone who is also far from regulated, not at all conscious, and they will trigger and bicker and blame. One might label, judge, and think the other person is abusive or toxic. No one is a label. People are where they are. They came to show you to do your work. You allowed them, accepted them, accepted all the red flags, didn't express yourself or your boundaries, through the fear of the loss of their love, their validation, and you remained and stayed because you feel unsafe, unworthy, and unloved from inside you. There are always two parts to a relationship.

I say less always accepts less and more will never accept less. The more you face yourself and do the work, the more you will match with the same resonating aspects.

The nervous system is far more intelligent than your mind. You are meeting the same level of relationship in someone else as the parent you got the least love from. You are trying to get those resonating unmet needs met. The nervous system seeks the familiar.

When we clear our lenses of perception, face our hurt and pain, break these loops, come back to a more regulated and worthy safe place within, a few things can happen.

We suddenly see others differently, more lovingly, because we have less unloved pain. We then find more compassion and acceptance and love instead of our criticism and blame.

Or we simply accept them for where they are, with no pointing, no victim narrative, no criticism, and no labeling, and walk away with love and compassion, to a new level of relating or a better relationship with ourselves for not clinging from our lack.

Many just keep moving from one partner to another, blaming and not facing their own stuff.

Some can come to us to show us to us, so we learn to love ourselves more, to just say no thanks.

Some come to show us to us, so we face ourselves to grow to a certain place and space and then grow apart. And some come to us to grow into the deepest and most intimate vulnerable relationship.

The latter is the rarest.

Two people have to be on the same page of education, regulation, and elevation to create a true love story.

I always say if you are in a relationship and read my books, you and your partner must both agree to read them. You are not there to parent, or coach, or be a therapist to each other. You are there to be a safe, regulated container of two who hold a space for each other to be able to openly and vulnerably take full responsibility and express their feelings without projection. This is courageous, authentic, and intimate relating.

Parents

Your greatest teachers and lessons are the people we label as parents. This is the core of your schoolwork.

Once, your parents were both little children who experienced a tough time, just like you, or most probably far worse. Regardless of your thoughts and beliefs, your resentments and unforgiving, your anger and even hate and bile, YOU hold onto it all, from you, by you, inside you. That's your experience you held onto from the past and are now soiling and poisoning your present with.

Your soul picked these souls, made contracts before birth, to teach you your biggest lessons. And those lessons are all that is being presented to you in the mirror and school of life.

They grew up, like you, and had no idea of how to

navigate their own experience, their own pain, their own hurt, their own blindness, not knowing how to emotionally regulate or regulate their nervous systems. They, like you, simply did their best and are doing their best, even if you wanted more from them or still do. That's where your unmet needs came from. You wanted them to be something you wanted, even though they had no ability or actual capabilities to. You literally wanted blood from a stone. And because they simply couldn't be how you wanted, you resented them, to varying degrees, and then felt unsafe, unworthy, and unloved. You made judgments against them and against yourself. And these feelings then became the weight of your unresolved inner issues.

Your first lesson in life is to find the utmost compassion for them, for how they were and how they still are. If not, we keep hold of the pain and poison, and it blocks our journey back to love. It's simply unloving to us to resent, to judge, to hold onto, and to have negative self-talk.

We just wanted to be loved the way we wanted. And they didn't know how to. And so, we protect our unloved hurt, pain, and shame with anger and resentments.

To feel all that pain, to face it and move through it, again and again, is how we resolve all the unresolved and come back to compassion and a greater understanding. But we spent our childhood pushing it all down, and it's been bursting, snapping, reacting, looping, pointing, and blaming ever since, to them, to your partners, to friends, to strangers, and anyone else who just happens to mirror you back to you. This is the core of the ammunition for our triggers.

The unloved just wants to feel loved again.

I always ask clients in my private Evolutionist sessions to tell me what their little child wanted from their parents in the words and language of their younger self.

I listen and hear their feelings and thoughts. It usually translates as they wanted to feel loved, met, seen, heard, and safe. They wanted to feel valued just as they were. They wanted attention, time, connection, to feel seen. That translates as a child feeling unsafe, unloved, and not good enough.

Then I ask them to tell me what they would say if they could loudly say to their parents today,

"Why can't you just _____?" Fill in the blank.

And this then spews out the same unmet needs still being triggered today as they had as a child. Their childhood resentments are still alive and well, blocking their whole adult life. And it is these answers, when reverse engineered and translated, that show us what we have to bring to ourselves. We have these deep inner childhood unmet needs trying to get met from people who still can't meet them, as well as from our present-day partners. A partner can be there to hold a safe space, but it's impossible for them to regulate our nervous systems or face and feel the feelings rising up to be worked through. That's for us to do.

We have to see our parents as little children who never read *The Map*, never had the operating manual, never faced their pain, or never even knew they were in pain. They are still those little children and not Mum and Dad. And it is these unmet needs we still want that play out in our lives and relationships. These are what are always triggered, that get angry, resent, snap, react. These feelings are the juice, the driving force, to face, to feel, to sit in, break the loops, move through, and heal.

Mum, why can't you just _____?

Dad, why can't you just_____?

Why can't you just love me?

Why can't you just listen to me?

Why can't you figure your life out so I can feel safe?

Why can't you just meet me where I am, see me for me?

Why can't you just validate me, praise me, be proud of me?

Why can't you make me feel safe?

These are a few I hear daily. They are sentences being driven by the pain and hurt of unmet needs. This unloved self, our unworthy self, our not good enough self, our unsafe self, wants them to still be what they can't be, what they never could be. Our teachers are showing us the deep work we have to do. This is where inner child work comes in, every time. These deep hurts and pains are also loops we can sit in and with, like an unconditional parent, and allow them to be felt.

When we are in contact or communication with our parents, these unresolved issues will be triggered within us to show us to us. The feeling will then join in with a narrative and either bicker, defend, feel unloved, unheard, not good enough, unsafe, shame, or frightened.

This is our homework in life. These are the feelings of then that we don't want to face, feel, and move through now. These loops of reactivity can all be broken like all others. It's the inner child presenting itself to be met, seen and heard, to have its feelings validated. They are feelings wrapped in old stories. They are not true stories. They are simply feelings. They are looping pains we code and download and keep alive. They are a program we are constantly not altering, not facing, not sitting in and dissolving.

What Happens

Parents or partners are how they are. (That's their stuff.)

WE ARE TRIGGERED (from within)

We have a feeling. (That's our stuff.)

We fall into our victim narrative, protect our hurt and pain and shame, and then point and project from it, react, criticize, defend, attack, bicker, complain, or blame.

Or we just wallow and shut down.

We don't feel the feeling, face it, move through it; we fall into it like a victim.

WE FEEL hurt and pain and shame or unsafe.

We feel like a little child all over again.

We have done this our whole lives. It's normal- ized behavior. The movies and TV show it, and our family did it and still do it. It's missing the point of the school of life. It's looping the loops of our pain again and again without breaking them.

Understanding this is one thing. Do not try to tell or teach others. Your work is yours. Most won't dare face themselves until their last gasp. That's their journey.

It is only in a relationship, parents or partners, when two people get on the same page of under- standing and take their full responsibility without projections that this can be faced and worked through together. That is a rarity.

Two wounded children who don't know they are wounded, don't know how to navigate and trans- late, and don't know how to hold a regulated space will simply bicker and project to protect their child- hood pain.

If the other does not wish to face their stuff, you

have to come into full acceptance of them where they are and do more work or love you that much more and walk away or express yourself, your boundaries, your feelings.

Inner child work:

Parents or partners are how they are. (That's their stuff.)

WE ARE TRIGGERED

We have a feeling. (That's our stuff.)

We notice the feeling in an instant and breathe to create space.

We observe.

We know this is our stuff.

We feel it. We know it's our inner child, an old loop trying to loop.

We can express to the teacher in the mirror, our parent or partner,

"Please allow me a moment. I am feeling triggered and would like to process."

We breathe. We ask the inner feeling.

"What are you feeling?" This validates, sees, and meets the inner pain.

We wait and listen for the voice inside of the inner child to tell us. "I feel not good enough, unloved, unworthy, not important. They don't listen to me. They don't care. I'm not stupid. I'm not bad, not wrong," shame, shame, shame. Or we could feel unsafe and want to snap from that feeling of fear and blame them for how we feel.

We listen to the narrative, to the feeling that is from our inner child. Then we express to it, "It's OK. I'm here. It's an old story. We know where this comes from. I'm here. I've got you. It's OK."

And we sit with the feeling without attaching to the narrative, without blame, and we feel it all the way through its duration, feeling it, breathing, regulating instead of falling off the cliff.

This is a practice. And it can be excruciating. We feel it until it loses its power and dissolves.

"It's OK. I'm here. It's OK. I've got you," I say to my little boy inside.

This can usually bring great tears. We get to be there for our pain like an unconditional parent.

These phrases and words are soothing and healing from within and bring us back to conscious awareness and not get lost in the old story and pain. We are learning to break these reactions, these loops, these patterns, that usually cause the effect of our falling unconscious and unaware and dysregulated and then get into conflict.

We can do this inner child work whenever we feel triggered, or down, or upset. We can also simply go into breaking loops.

We see and relate to others through the lenses of our old hurt, shame, and pain. When we face these feelings, again and again, dissolve them, others magically change. It's not them; most of the time, it's how we feel, believe, and perceive.

As Wayne Dyer said, "When we change the way we see things, the things we see change."

I went to a college many years ago to study spiritual psychology—the University of Santa Monica. Back then, it was all in person. There were no books. We simply facilitated each other and learned to listen and to share and to face our stuff, openly and vulnerably. It literally turned me inside out and upside down and opened a whole can of dark worms.

After the first year, a girl stood up and shared her story. She said that a year ago, before the college, she was at a job. She said she hated her job and hated everyone who worked there. She then said that after a year of college, of facing her stuff, doing her work, she was still at the same job but loved her job and also loved everyone else there. She said the only thing that had changed was her.

This story always makes me emotional. I did my best where I was on my journey and have since done my very best and more. And I have never stopped facing and owning my darkness.

The Gravitational Pull and Tsunami Force of Falling from Grace

We only fall into our suffering, our unconsciousness, our hurt and pain, off the edge of our cliff, when the force and pull of the old loops drag us downwardly inside. This is the opposite of the elevated higher self who observes and watches, detached. We have been avoiding and not facing our pain, deflecting and protecting it, blaming, pointing and projecting from it, and hiding and soothing it our whole life. The last thing we want to do is face it and feel it. The force and pull we feel is just this. It's an old childhood survival mechanism we have constantly lived and played out, unaware, on autopilot, for the duration of our lives. This is a habit, an addiction, a default setting that does not want to feel the pain. Unfortunately, if we don't face and feel it all the way through its duration, we keep cementing it. The process is to create a regulated nervous system, a stronger conscious awareness, constantly dissolving and resolving our old pain again and again, as we expand and elevate and evolve from within, moment to moment. We either cement our karma, looping it, stagnating in it, or we cremate it and rise from its ashes to regulate and elevate from it.

This pull and force is very much the hardest aspect to face. It can literally feel like we are dying. We won't die. We will simply die to that old part of us, the old way of being, the old reactions, protections, projections, patterns, and programs, and how we used to download our code, loop our loops. This is a practice and process, not an event. You have looped the same reactions, protecting the same pains, again and again, your whole life. Your operating systems all join in together to work together to keep the familiar being familiar and safe, even if it's an unsafe feeling. And they are all set on their default and do an amazing job of looping themselves into themselves. This work is not easy or for those who are weak of willpower. This is determined, courageous, disciplined self-inquiry and self-facing work.

This force and pull to react, to fall unconscious, is the same as facing our need for soothing. We have a constant of potential opportunities to fall or rise above. As I wrote in *The Map*, it's a game of snakes and ladders.

Example

Someone you know, a parent, partner, or friend, or anyone else, says something, and you feel the need to defend, to criticize, to attack back, to react. The reaction is your protection of your old hurt and pain and mostly shame. You don't ever stop to feel it. You normally just react to protect it.

The feeling is the way through, the way to dissolve the old pain, the old hurt, the old shame. But we don't know this of ourselves. So, the reactions bicker, argue, criticize, blame, judge, complain, and can even become loud, aggressive, and violent, depending on the depth of hurt, shame, and pain you don't want to face and feel.

Much of what we feel is a mild to serious deep pain of shame not wanting to be faced. It can also be a deeply unsafe feeling that fights to feel safe.

Example

(I thought about this next example and if I should keep it in the book. I decided it would serve others to save them the same reactions, to save them their own pain, to save them hurting another person's feelings, and to maybe save relationships. This was a huge humbling lesson for me, and I know it will be for many.)

Several years ago, an ex was now dating other men. After being a blind bleeding beggar and a people pleaser, being there in between every other man she was with, I had told her it was not healthy for me to be a friend while she was dating others. I broke off contact, expressing this. This was my stuff to face. This was my clinging to some form of validation from my deep abandonment pain and shame.

Three months later, after no contact, I found out from someone else that she was going to come to my little town and bring her newest man. Rage came up, and I ranted in texts saying she was not welcome in my town and to stay away from my house. I spewed my projected hurt and pain and was simply raging to cover up my childhood shame.

Soon enough, I sat with myself, and I faced my hurt and pain, did the work, and cried and cried deeply with my inner child about not feeling loved, about not feeling good enough, about feeling stupid, bad, and wrong, and thinking and believing the narrative that this other man was better than me. That was my deep shame from childhood of always being squashed down by others, being ridiculed for this or that, for feeling deeply unloved and not good enough.

This was all coming to the surface to be faced and felt and moved into and through. It was about everything else but her and him. It was all about the pain of my oldest and deepest shame. This rage, abandonment rage, is why people can do physical harm to others. It's literally a flooding of the brain of chemicals. The body is trying to protect itself from feeling very old, deep excruciating pain. This is the past coming up, being presented to be faced, to feel, to heal. But we don't know this. We loop the hurt feelings in a victim narrative. It seems like the other people are hurting us, their actions. No, it's not. Others are being how they are. That's the what is of it all. How we feel is all our old hurt, our old shame.

I sat with it, and in it, again and again, every time I felt the rage come up. The narratives of revenge, of spite, of vengeance were how my parents were for decades after their divorce. I was programmed to feel rage, even though I didn't know it, on top of my own pain of my own shame and abandonment. Years of knowledge or courses and classes and reading books and many plant medicines couldn't do this work, just me, the pain, and feeling it, moving into and through it, again and again.

Forgive me for I knew not.

Forgive them for they know not.

I faced my pain so many times asking my inner child how he felt. "No one loves me," he would cry. He was the three-year-old boy hiding in a dark cupboard crying and hoping the violence would not come to him. He felt so unloved, so stupid and unworthy. He was the little boy whose mother continually screamed and beat him. He was the little boy who was ridiculed constantly, who felt so much shame, so unloved.

I got to see my hurt and pain and shame and do the deepest work on myself. And from that whole journey, I regulated and elevated and moved through so much that I now assist so many other people in seeing their hurt, their pain.

That circumstance was my greatest teacher that finally showed me to me, for me to face myself.

I literally took to this deeper work due to all my abandonment pains from that one past relationship and the patterns of a lifetime that also came up, again and again, after many repeated reactions of the same in other past relationships.

This was genius. I was now capable, regulated, and conscious enough and ready to face the pain.

I could have just continued dating, having flings, find a band aid for my blind, bleeding beggar of abandonment, like most do, or go to drinking, hiding, escaping, soothing, resenting, and hating, being a victim, and being angry, etc. I faced every aspect of what I never faced. It was a lot of pain and hurt and shame. It would continually present itself to see if I had mastered it. This is what happens. It spirals back again and again, just to see if we have gained real mastery. There would be some anger, some narrative, some resentment, and I just did the inner child work, just faced the pain, and cried again and again as I continually broke the loops of shame.

This was an ongoing work for a long time. Eventually there was nothing left but love. The resentment was covering up all my deep shame of feeling like no one loved me and I was just wrong, no good, bad. None of which was true. Just my homework. Just stuck feelings and the story I projected onto others.

Eventually, two years after the rage tirade of texts, I sent a voice note sending love. This was my greatest teacher in the mirror who allowed me to see so much pain I was running from. The genius of this work is just that.

My mother hated my father her whole life. They both continually spewed spite and anger toward each other, even though they both remarried. My whole life it was a bitter resentment from them both about each other. Then, one day, my mother died suddenly of a heart attack. My father called me. He was crying. His words?

"No matter what, I always loved your mother."
I'm crying now just writing this. His protective
mask, his armor, fell, crumbled, and his heart spoke
his truth. He had his own pain, and so did she. They
didn't know how to find their way back to love. I
understand. I couldn't either. And my work took
me through what I had to, to come to back to love
from all my protective layers.

To love, unconditionally is the most heroic thing
you can do.

Recap

I breathe. I regulate. I strengthen my conscious
awareness by creating space for me to catch my
old reactions and not fall off the edge of the cliff
into my dysregulations, into the feelings and narratives. I breathe, face my feelings, feel my feelings, be
with my feelings, don't narrate a story from them,
or point a story outwardly to life and others. I feel
it all, sit with it all, don't get pulled into it, and just
allow it to travel its journey as I feel it and observe
it. I keep my awareness, I burn in it, I continue and
watch it dissolve, and I breathe. This is breaking
the loops. I remain aware, conscious even as it

subsides. I sit with the space. I feel the space. I am mastering myself. I am rewiring neural pathways, subconscious programs and patterns, and regulating my nervous system, while not uploading the same old codes of me. I watch and wait until it is clear and calm. I close the space with gratitude and a knowing of elevation and heroic growth. I slay my dragons and demons, my darkness, and in lighten my weight, loop by loop, breaking them, until this becomes my second nature. This can last as short as seconds to even hours of vigilance. We can use and add inner child work to assist and be there for the hurt and pain, the need to protect it. Eventually, you will literally be able to break a loop in an instant.

As a child, I didn't know how to process my hurt feelings. And my parents were also pretty blind to their own abilities. I had zero actual education in my ability to regulate my nervous system or my emotions. I then blindly attempted, as best I could, to figure it out, to navigate my pain. I didn't want to feel the feelings, or have them, so I just kind of pushed them down, hid them, and then created a narrative around them and about me. I'm no good, bad, wrong, stupid, unsafe, unloved, not good enough, and no one loves me. I did this. And this is a lot of pain and shame. I lived with a whole childhood of pushed-down hurt feelings as well as a well-rehearsed and reactive looping script about myself. This then played out when I felt triggered, felt upset. That's the actuality of what was going on. I played my play, re-acted my reactions, felt my feelings, narrated my story, blamed my blames, soothed, and covered it all up.

Nothing I feel is actually new, it's just me looping old loops.

This is all my old stuff asking to be finally faced, felt, moved through, and dissolved. If I had no stuff, if I were emotionally regulated from a child, no one could reflect anything back to me. I would simply have compassion for their own hurt and pain pointing at me, speaking to me, reacting at me. Triggers and upsets would be a rarity.

The other is simply a mirror.

They show me to me.

I feel my old stuff.

From there, I loop or I break the loops.

My whole life, if a girlfriend would tell me they loved me, I would feel terror and shut down. This was because my mother would tell me she loved me, and soon enough beat me and scream at me. Love was very unsafe. Love would hurt me. Unaware of this, I would protect myself from being hurt. My deep feeling of no one loves me would now actually come true because the more I shut down, the more I pushed girlfriends away. Eventually, they left me. And bingo, I felt like no one loved me. I had to do this work and face my old shutdown, my terror of love hurting me. Now, being told I'm loved is a sweetness to receive without any fear.

Everyone Else

Just like you, everyone else is mostly clueless to the blindness of their operating systems. Expecting others to be how you want them to be is rather ignorant. Trying to change others to fit how you need them to be comes from a feeling inside of our unmet needs. What lens you see through, unloved, unsafe, unworthy, not good enough, not important, is what and how you feel and see. These are our lenses of perceptions. And that is what you will attract in others to see and feel about yourself. Most of us play the victim and point at others. We blame them from our feelings. We are actually seeing them through the lenses of our unresolved issues. As we resolve them, we see very differently. As we break loops, we gain power and strength to keep breaking loops. As we do this we expand, regulate, elevate, resolve, dissolve, and evolve to higher and more expansive resonating spaces of consciousness within.

Final Words

The Map and this book are simple and yet very powerful intellectual understandings. They may shift your perceptions to a degree. But without the practice of the living regulation meditation, breathing, strengthening conscious awareness and breaking the loops, inner child work, and non-reactivity, we will continue to code, download, react, fall off the edge of the cliff, and replay the pain, narrate from it, blame from it, judge and criticize from it, and loop the same old same, again and again. We either live in the victim's story or the hero's glory. This is our courageous new life choice. This is a determined and disciplined journey of facing it all, moment to moment.

The idea is to become the conscious awareness space and not keep getting attached to the stuff we have always stuffed into it, our neurosis and insecurity, our triggered upsets and disturbs. As we process and practice, we find our triggers become less in duration and easier to move through, our reactions diminish to a fraction, and we reduce our overall distress, dis-ease, and disturbs of life. This is the constant of coming to contentment and peace.

The Map is the mirror that shows where you strayed, and the compass pointing you home. The Operating Manual is the lantern in your hand, guiding each step as you return.

Free Handwriting

This is a great tool to use when stuck in any deep feeling. Get ten pieces of paper. Find a quiet space for fifteen minutes. You now rant write, put your pain to the page. You don't care about the handwriting or even think about what you're writing. You let it just flow out. Let whatever comes out onto the page to do so. It can be crude, rude, nasty, vile, however and whatever, just allow it. It might even make no sense but just write whatever comes from the unconscious. A few things can happen, but don't look for, expect, or force them. Sometimes we might just run out of steam and feel we unblocked the feelings that were stuck. Sometimes we might write something, and it comes out really profound and shifts us to a level of deeper understanding about the stuck feelings. Sometimes it can reveal deeper aspects from our childhood, and we can burst into tears and release the pain. Just allow this to flow, to rant, to rage on the page. Then after, burn the pages. Do not burn down the house. Please be wise, safe, and careful about this.

All we experience are feelings, thoughts, and narratives. They are the ethers of our being and seeing. They are simply a visceral looping of code downloading that seems to be real. It's a trick, a cosmic joke.

Nothing is real. Nothing to get hung up about.

This moment is the only moment your conscious awareness should be on. And whatever arises from within you can be detached from, dissolved, or moved through. You are continually authoring and creating from this space. What you decide to loop is up to you. What you believe is how you perceive and how you then receive in the mirror.

I made this book as small and compact as possible to give as much as I could in a small read. I repeat myself on purpose, to truly assist and shift the messages into a deeper level.

I wish you well on your journey. This work is life work, not a final destination.

I have incredible amounts of free content on Instagram. Take in the intellectual understanding and actualize and embody each moment of every moment until it becomes the new operating system of you.

Sending you much love.

All my books can be seen on
my website with direct links to Amazon:

www.thepoweroflove.art

A mantra prayer I like to sing to myself:

Thank you for the love.

Thank you for the health.

Thank you for the miracles,

the magic, and the wealth.

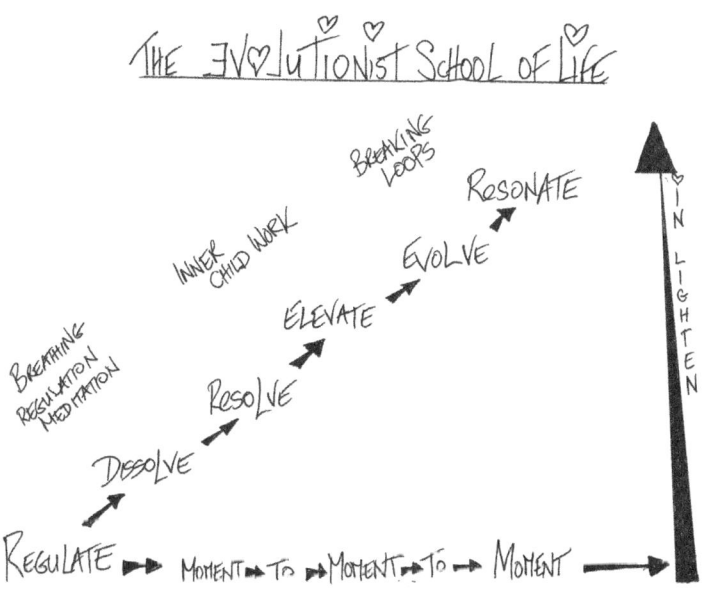

Made in the USA
Coppell, TX
21 September 2025

60325289R00090